CONTENTS

REDCOATS, YANKEES AND ALLIES

A History of the Uniforms, Clothing and Gear of the British Army in the Lake George – Lake Champlain Corridor 1755-1760

Brenton C. Kemmer

Illustrations by Joe Lee

Heritage Books, Inc.

Copyright 1998

Brenton C. Kemmer
Illustrations by Joe Lee

Another Heritage Book by the author:

Freemen, Freeholders and Citizen Soldiers:
An Organizational History of Colonel Jonathan Bagley's Regiment, 1755-176

Published 1998 by

HERITAGE BOOKS, INC.
1540E Pointer Ridge Place
Bowie, Maryland 20716
1-800-398-7709
www.heritagebooks.com

ISBN 0-7884-0905-0

A Complete Catalog Listing Hundreds of Titles
On History, Genealogy, and Americana
Available Free Upon Request

* Many soilders wore Regular non issue clothes No rank shown Worn to show no Rank. Protection and from weather and very worn Not Replaced - Civilian clothing worn by Union Soildiers - Worn out - dirty often not warm nore protection from weather.

British uniforms
were distictive-
mended - replaced
Officers #1
enlisted men seldome
dressed to tell rank,
etc.

Officers bought
their uniformans.
Much mismached
of uniforms.
uniforms were not
worn by volenteers
British uniforms were
High class-
Revolution uniforms
worn by Officers
were Paid for by
the wearer.

ACKNOWLEDGMENTS

The research for this work has not just been a recent project but rather an accumulation of research and materials for the past decade and a half. It was during that time that I became acquainted with several friends who began to openly share their interest and research on the British soldiery in North America during the Seven Years' War. Over this time, I have been lucky enough to get to know many other knowledgeable historians with interests on many different topics of this world conflict. It was shortly after completion of _Freemen, Freeholders, and Citizen Soldiers,_ that I began to realize that there was a need to share my research and shared information on other units in the British Army.

My reasoning for the writing of this uniform history was not to produce an all encompassing history of uniforms of the British Army or just a thumbnail sketch of some of the regiments' clothing. I, as other historians, had noticed a void in uniform histories, especially geographical in-depth studies. Therefore I have composed _Redcoats, Yankees, and Allies._ I have taken the all-important Lake George–Lake Champlain corridor as the geographic area for this history. It was this natural route that the armies of the Seven Years' War utilized annually to subdue the French in North America. Again in the American Revolution, this corridor proved to be one of the most important routes followed by British and rebel alike. In utilizing this area, this study is limited to only the units of the redcoat (grenadier, regular, light infantry), Yankee (provincials and rangers), and allies (Native Americans) who served in this corridor during the war. Other regiments and locations have been left for future volumes or other authors.

In finalizing my research, I relied on several living history friends who portray regiments within this study. These individuals were kind enough to share their research and knowledge on their unit's histories. In some cases, these men saved me leg work and, in other cases, they were able to help me fill some voids in my findings. I would like to thank John Eric Nelson of the Connecticut Regiment, Eric Lorenzen of the New York Regiment, Jeremy Muraski of the New Hampshire Regiment, Tim Todish of Rogers' Rangers, and Barton Redmon of the 60th Regiment of Foot.

I would like to thank several individuals for reading my manuscript. Without the insight of others, it is difficult to diversify one's work. Acknowledgment goes to Darlene Lee, Betty Kemmer, Maureen Talaricco, Tim Veryzer, and Kim Frazho.

Two people were the main readers of this manuscript. I chose a friend, fellow historian, writer, and living historian, Dr. Todd Harburn to critique this manuscript historically. Todd had some good suggestion in finalizing this work and also has added in the information of the regulars and, specifically, the 60th Regiment of Foot. I must thank Ted Goll, a fellow educator for his help as the primary proofreader.

The artist of this work has been my personal friend for several years now and has proven his professionalism as is commonplace in all his work. Joe Lee has taken my notes and designs and created the enclosed artistic works. Joe's and his wife's friendship has been much appreciated by my family through research trips taken together the past few summers.

For many years now, I have been privy to participate and observe demonstrations, lectures, and educational programs at historic Seven Years' War sites around North America. All these sites have done an excellent job at helping their visitors understand the clothing, gear, and equipment of the Seven Years' War soldier. It is because of these excellent interpretive programs that I dedicate this book to the Seven Years' War sites of North America. It is my hope that this book will further their efforts to enhance the historical education and interest of their visitors. I would like to extend my thanks to the dedicated employees and directors of these sites.

Part I:

<u>HISTORY OF THE CORRIDOR</u>

His Majesty has been graciously pleased to signify that he has nothing more at Heart then to repair the Losses and Disappointments of the last inactive and unhappy Campaign, and by vigorous and extensive Efforts, to avert, by the blessing of GOD on his Arms, the Dangers impending on North-America, and not doubting by all his faithful and brave Subjects here, will cheerfully co-operate with, and second to the utmost, the large Expense, and extraordinary Succors, supplied by the Kingdom of Great-Britain, for their Provinces of the Massachusetts-Bay, New-Hampshire, Rhode-Island, Connecticut, New-York, and New-Jersey, are of themselves, well able to furnish at least TWENTY THOUSAND Men, to join A Body of the KING's Forces for invading Canada, and carrying War into the Heart of the Enemy's Possessions.[1]

The Seven Years' War is monumental in the military history of the world. Unfortunately, historians have not dedicated a proper proportion of study to this particular war. Here in America, this was the last in a string of colonial French and Indian Wars; it was the training ground for the future conflict between Britain and her colonies–the American Revolution.

---

[1] "A Proclamation by His Majesty King George for the Raising of a Provincial Army," 1758. Photocopy, courtesy of Jerry Olson, in Author's Private Collection, Houghton Lake, Mich.

Even the topographical area in which much of the Seven Years' War and the Revolution was fought is congruent. Strategically, the Lake George–Lake Champlain Corridor proved to be the all important battleground in colonial America. Yearly, the British Forces in America would attempt to surge northward in a massive invasion of New France through this natural avenue.   One of the major learning experiences of this war was the uniforming and equipping of the thousands of troops serving for King George II.
(See *Map 1.*)

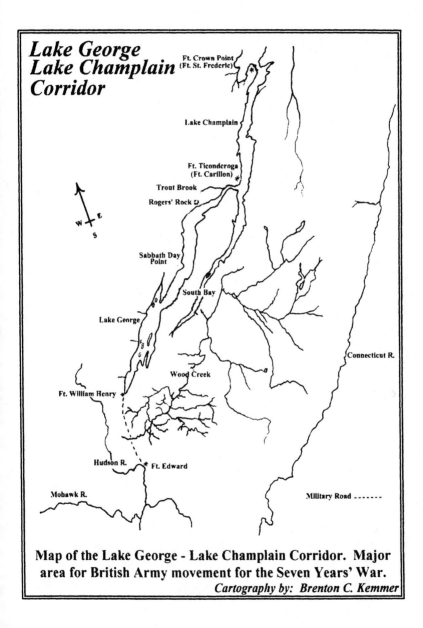

Map of the Lake George - Lake Champlain Corridor. Major area for British Army movement for the Seven Years' War.
Cartography by: Brenton C. Kemmer

Map 1

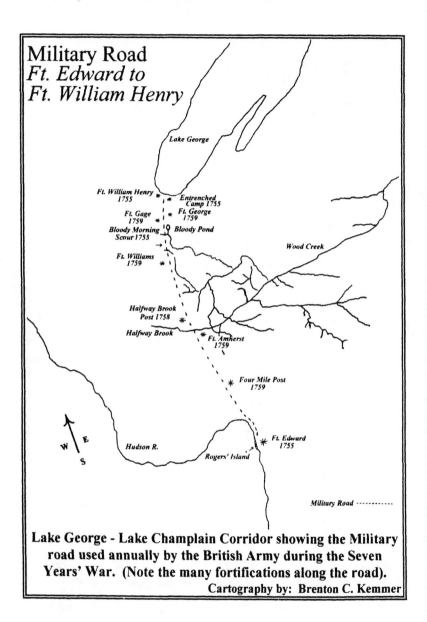

Lake George - Lake Champlain Corridor showing the Military road used annually by the British Army during the Seven Years' War. (Note the many fortifications along the road).

Cartography by: Brenton C. Kemmer

Map 2

THE CAMPAIGN OF 1755

In 1755, the main thrust into the Lake George area was to be unique. A New Yorker who had been born in Ireland, with no battle experience and next to no military study was chosen commander. William Johnson led an all-provincial army north from Albany to capture the French Fort St. Frédéric on Lake Champlain. Johnson was to be at the head of a mixed troop of Massachusetts, Connecticut, New York, New Hampshire, and Rhode Island soldiers, along with their women and children camp followers. As well as these Americans, Johnson had with him 250-300 Native Americans. He started out with fifty and was reinforced by 200-250 more Indians on his northern quest for victory. The majority of these Indians, as proves true for the rest of the war, were Mohawks from Johnson's home valley and the Oneidas just west of his estate in the Mohawk Valley. There were, as well, about fifty natives from Stockbridge, Massachusetts, called Mohicans, and several Mohegans from Connecticut in the provincial regiments. Johnson's token redcoat was his assigned engineer, William Eyre of the 44th Regiment of Foot.

The first objective of Johnson and his Yankees, Indians and camp followers was to advance and set up a fortified supply post on the upper Hudson River just south of Lac St. Sacrement (soon to be renamed Lake George by William Johnson). His army congregated in three waves at a small, fortified trade post, Fort Lydius. Here they built store houses, powder magazines, and started a stockade. Shortly after arriving and setting up his headquarters on the island in the Hudson across from the new fortifications, Johnson sent north detachments toward South Bay to the east of the lake and to the southern end of Lac St. Sacrement to build two thirty-foot-wide supply roads and select a location for a forward post toward Fort St. Frédéric (see *Map 2*). At about that time, the majority of Johnson's Indian allied contingent arrived under the leadership of the sachem, King Hendrick. A native youth of thirteen, Joseph Brant, who was to be important in the Revolution, accompanied the Mohawks.

By July, the camp followers had earned a dubious reputation. Col. Phineas Lyman of one of the Connecticut regiments was appalled by some of the followers, especially from New York and Rhode Island, and asked Johnson to deny them from the camp. Johnson acknowledged the problem but also expressed his knowledge of the importance of the wives and their necessity for washing and mending for the troops. Eventually, the majority of the New Englanders won out, citing the followers as a burden, and they were removed from camp and sent back to Albany, the place of rendezvous (see Figures 1 and 2).

Engineer Eyre laid out a plan for the fort and construction expanded on Fort Lydius. At that time, to honor the monarchy, Johnson renamed the new fort, Fort Edward. The forward detachments, cutting roads as they advanced, decided against the South Bay area, and their efforts were concentrated on the base of Lac St. Sacrement. Eyre was sent forward from Fort Edward with a large detachment, and started clearing land for a fort. Shortly after the clearing, he sent out a scouting party toward South Bay, who ran across the trail of a large French and Indian party heading toward Fort Edward.

Johnson decided to send two separate detachments of five hundred men each to try and intercept or cut off the enemy. King Hendrick expressed, as did many of the provincial field officers, that this was too small of a party. A council of war was convened; the members decided to combine the detachments.

THE BLOODY MORNING SCOUT. On the morning of September 8, Col. Ephraim Williams of one of the Massachusetts regiments led out two hundred Indians, his own regiment, a Connecticut regiment, and the Rhode Island

Fig. 1. Hundreds of women and children camp followers traversed the Lake George - Lake Champlain Corridor following their respective regiments washing, mending, cooking, nursing, and seeing to all the troops' needs. Notice the mixture of women's and soldiers' clothing picked up by these followers.

Fig. 2. There was a great diversity of types of women camp followers. The majority were related to the soldiers but others ranged from officers' mistresses to prostitutes. The lady on the left is obviously an officer's wife. The woman on the right is the type of follower looked down upon by the New England Yankees.

regiment under Lt. Col. Edward Cole. King Hendrick, old, obese, and on a horse lent him by Johnson, led his two hundred natives in single file, advancing down the road to Fort Edward. Next came Ephraim Williams and his Massachusetts regiment, followed by the Connecticut men, and in the rear were the Rhode Islanders, marching five to six abreast.

Good reconnaissance told the French under the command of Baron Dieskau of the advance of Williams' party, and Dieskau placed his Indians and Canadian militia in the wooded ridges on the flanks of the new road. He positioned his French regulars on the road. His orders were to hold fire until his regulars fired, which would place the entire provincial column within his ambush.

Some of Dieskau's Indians were Caughnawaga – Canadian Mohawks who felt obliged to warn the New York Iroquois League Mohawks. A shot rang out, and, in an Iroquois tongue, a French allied Indian yelled out, "Who goes there?" Hendrick replied, "We are the six confederate Indian nations, the heads and superiors of all Indian nations."[2] More words were exchanged, and a young Mohawk behind King Hendrick fired on the enemy spokesman, and musket fire erupted from both sides immediately killing forty of Hendrick's Indians. Hendrick rolled off his horse, possibly wounded, and took to the woods with the other fleeing allied Indians. Unfortunately, Hendrick could not keep up, became disoriented, and ran directly into a temporary enemy camp of women and boys too young to take part in the ambush. Immediately, the boys charged old Hendrick, killing him with their tomahawks, spears, and bows and arrows. After that, they scalped and mutilated poor Hendrick.

The front half of the Massachusetts regiment also had entered into the ambush, and there was mass carnage upon the first volleys. With the remnants of Williams' regiment

---

[2] Arthur L. Perry, *Origins in Williamstown* (New York: Charles Scribner's Sons, 1894) 346.

retreating in horror through them, the rest of the column became frantic, and a route commenced. The Rhode Islanders started a semi-orderly retreat, attempting to hold the French at bay, while Johnson fortified his position. After the initial attack, Dieskau's Indians and many Canadians began looting and scalping the downed bodies, and Dieskau was not able to wrangle them to rejoin his attack. Dieskau with his regulars, and those others he could convince, continued their firing advance.

Johnson, hearing the distant gun fire, started to fortify his camp by placing felled trees, wagons, and boats around his perimeters. Johnson sent Col. Nathan Whiting out with his Connecticut regiment to support the retreating detachment. Col. Whiting did a valiant job with well ordered volley fire while the other routing Yankees poured into Johnson's camp. Fright and chaos almost took over the provincials as their officers galloped up and down the lines yelling orders at their regiments, beating them with the flats of their swords, and preparing them for the onslaught of the French. Johnson's cannons were placed in the middle of the road on the lines, and William Eyre was placed in charge of their usage.

Dieskau hit first the center, and Eyre's cannons ripped roadways through the French regulars. Then, Dieskau concentrated on the flanks individually. Unfortunately, he was not able to bolster many Canadians or Indians to help his siege. Consequently, by the time he hit the second flank and Eyre trained his guns to that flank in support, his offense was exhausted, and the Yankees hurtled their makeshift breastworks and charged the French retreat, capturing Dieskau.

When shots from the morning battle were heard at Fort Edward, a detachment was sent toward South Bay to try and support or cut off the French. This detachment surprised a party of looting Canadians and Indians and wreaked havoc on the enemy; then swung west to Johnson's camp.

After things calmed down, Johnson held a council of war, and it was decided to move the place for the fort slightly to the west.   For the remainder of the 1755 campaign, Johnson, though restricted to his tent because of a wounded hip from the battle, had work parties at both Fort Edward and the newly renamed Lake George (Lac St. Sacrement) in honor of King George II. Both forts had major construction through the fall as well as constant false alarms by guards and scouting parties. Johnson's Indians primarily left after the battle, and he rarely had more than a dozen in camp at once, excepting the Massachusetts and Connecticut Indians. Without his Mohawks for reconnaissance, Johnson started using parties of provincials and ranging companies from the colonial regiments for scouting.   Most of these parties either brought back false information or were scared back to camp so quickly that they were of no use.   Two of the most successful colonial ranger units were Capt. Robert Rogers' ranging company of Col. Joseph Blanchard's New Hampshire regiment and Capt. Israel Putnam's Connecticut ranging company. Rogers and Putnam, as well as many of their men, were used to the rigors of the wilderness and started to be Johnson's premier reconnaissance units.

Finally, after a long autumn filled with back-breaking construction work and nerve-wracking anxiety, the majority of Johnson's army left for home. The newly named Fort William Henry had become usable in only about one and a half months. On November 27, Johnson and his army left Col. Jonathan Bagley of Massachusetts to command the garrisons at Fort Edward and Fort William Henry.   Bagley was to directly command Fort William Henry but had only 206 of the 402 Massachusetts, Connecticut, and New York garrison promised him.

THE CAMPAIGN OF 1756

That winter brought a new tradition of winter campaigning. It had been the practice of armies up to that time to dismiss or quarter troops in towns during the winter. That year, Bagley continually sent scouting and terrorist parties to roam north up Lake George and harass the enemy camps at Fort Carillon and Fort St. Frédéric. William Shirley, Governor of Massachusetts and Commander of British Forces in America, ordered one of Bagley's ranger units, Rogers' New Hampshire men, "to distress the French and their allies by sacking, burning, and destroying their houses, barns, barracks, canoes, bateaux, etc."[3] Under these orders, Rogers proceeded with a reign of woodland terrorism throughout the war through all seasons. Shirley's and Bagley's other American rangers kept constant reconnaissance on the enemy positions through the seasons' snowfall.

By March 1756, British commanders were taking notice of the American rangers and ordered Robert Rogers to recruit for a new company.   By June, recruits from Massachusetts, Connecticut, New York, New Hampshire and Rhode Island, as well as American rangers and Indians began to assemble at Albany to head north again to campaign against the French forts on Lake George and Lake Champlain.   At that time, Rogers was ordered to raise a third company, and a company of thirty Stockbridge Mohicans under Capt. Jacob Cheeksaunkun was placed under Rogers' command. This and his existing companies were to be an independent corps under pay and supply of the King separate from the colonial rangers. This corps was to be designated as His Majesty's Independent

---

[3] *Reminiscences of the French War, Robert Rogers' Journal and a Memoir of General Stark* (Hereafter cited as *Rogers' Journal*) (Freedom, N.H.: The Freedom Historical Society, 1988) 14.

Companies of American Rangers. The other Mohicans on that campaign were within the Massachusetts regiments, and five joined a New York regiment.

With the congregation of regiments and the problems of providing and moving supplies safely, several commands were given. First, orders were given that all regiments were to enlist or appoint sutlers or persons to supply them with their necessities. In order to transport the supplies from sutlers and the King's stores, wagons and wagoners were recruited to move goods to the campaign front. Another important transportation system, especially for using the Mohawk and Hudson Rivers, were bateaux. Like the British, the French had partisan war, scouting, and terrorists units ranging south into the areas of Fort William Henry, Fort Edward, and even toward Albany. Shirley, in order to try and reduce the number of covering parties needed to protect the transportation, ordered the recruitment of two thousand men, armed them specifically as armed bateaux men, and placed them under the command of Col. John Bradstreet. In order to transport stores up the Hudson and to advance an army forward from Fort William Henry, Bagley had gangs of soldiers/carpenters building three sloops and hundreds of whaleboats and bateaux.

That spring, William Johnson, because of his success against Dieskau in 1755, was made a Baron and was commissioned Superintendent of the Six Nations of the Iroquois and other northern tribes in America. Unfortunately, he, as did the colonial governors, had difficulty pushing levies toward the front.

The worst problem of 1756 was caused by the new Commander of North America, Lord Loudon. Loudon dictated a royal order that all field officers of colonial troops when serving with British regulars were to rank as senior captains, no matter what their actual rank. That ruling placed any British senior captains superior to all provincial majors, colonels, and generals. Some of the levies had enlisted under specifications of serving under their own officers, and most Yankee field officers belligerently were not going to be dictated into subordination.   Loudon's plan was a great disaster, and he tried written and then face-to-face negotiations with Gen. John Winslow of Massachusetts, commander of the troops already in place at the front. When specifically asked by Loudon if colonials would serve with the redcoats, Winslow made no firm guarantees.

With most provincial levies at the front, part of the 35th, 42nd, 44th, 48th, and 60th Regiments of Foot were marched to Fort Edward. Extreme tensions prevailed, and upon receiving word of the defeat of the garrison at Fort Oswego falling to the French, Loudon ordered Gen. Daniel Webb of the 48th Regiment of Foot, then commander of Fort Edward, to set aside the campaign against Fort Carillon and Fort St. Frédéric and to start defensive maneuvers at Lake George.

That autumn, Johnson's negotiations with the Indians produced only meager native assistance.   In September, George Croghan, one of Sir William's Indian agents, arrived at Fort Edward with sixty-nine Mohawks and Oneidas. Then, a month later, Johnson arrived at Fort William Henry with sixty-three Indians. Also that fall, Webb ordered a roster of camp followers to be made, by regiment.   That allowed the commanders correct numbers in order to prepare ration allowances, and provided a valuable count of women available for duties in the camps and hospitals.

Just before the army headed into winter quarters, Loudon gave orders to Rogers to augment his ranger corps by raising two new companies under the command of Capt. Humphrey Hobbs and Capt. Thomas Speakman. Then, in December, the majority of the Yankees and some of the redcoats were dismissed or sent into winter quarters while a few provincials, many of the army's rangers and four hundred redcoats, all under William Eyre, were sent up to Fort William Henry to relieve the provincial garrison. The redcoat garrisons for Fort

William Henry and Fort Edward were to be soldiers of the 44th and 48th Regiments of Foot.

THE CAMPAIGN OF 1757

The year 1757 was destined to spawn multiple military disasters for the British on the Lake George–Lake Champlain Corridor. On January 15, Rogers headed north to capture prisoners with a force of seventy-four rangers and volunteers. On January 21, they spotted a sleigh traveling over the ice on Lake Champlain. Rogers sent Lt. John Stark and twenty of his force forward to intercept it, but, shortly after, eight more sleighs appeared, and Rogers could not warn or call back the detail. Prisoners were taken from the first sleigh, and then the other sleighs arrived, and the British detachment was ordered into the woods. Rogers realized they could not overtake the sleighs and that the sleighs were heading directly to Fort Carillon where reinforcements would be upon Rogers immediately. His force retreated to where they had previously made fires, rekindled them and dried their muskets in preparation for a possible battle. Then they started heading back to Fort William Henry. They reached a rise, and the front of Rogers' column was hit with a barrage of gun fire and fell back into the remainder of the column. Men became separated, and a running battle on snowshoes ensued with a far superior force of French, Canadians, and Indians. Rogers' force received and inflicted large percentages of casualties. The fight continued till dark when the remnant of the rangers dispersed and made their way in the night back to Fort William Henry.

In March, the garrison of Fort William Henry, heavily manned by Irish troops, planned a party for St. Patrick's Day. Most of the Irish became drunk, as the French had anticipated. Commander Eyre gave orders to the non-Irish to stay alert and remain sober. That proved good thinking, because at 2 A.M. on March 17, the William Henry garrison was alerted by the sounds of axes, which meant that the French were making scaling ladders. For four days, primarily at night, the French and their allies tried to take the fort with small arms fire and burning. The primary losses were the burning of a sloop, some bateaux, storehouses, huts, and a woodpile. The French could not succeed with their scaling ladders versus the grapeshot being fired from the fort.

Spring brought two new companies to Rogers' command. One company, which was made up of New Jersey men, was commanded by Captain Burgin. The second company was made up of New Hampshire men, and was commanded by Captain Shepard. Another New Jersey company of provincial rangers was formed that spring. That unit was the second company of the New Jersey Frontier Guards under the command of Hezekiah Dunn. The company was not held at New Jersey, but rather was sent to Lake George. Putnam's rangers were still at the front as well, and were quartered on the island in the Hudson across from Fort Edward. The island was later known as Rogers' Island. Like many ranger companies, Putnam's had Indians in their ranks–Stockbridge Mohicans from Massachusetts.

Loudon, in order to help with the constant problems in using Indians and rangers for reconnaissance and terrorism, formed a cadet company of volunteers from the redcoats to train under Robert Rogers, learning his techniques in woods warfare. The men were then to return to the regulars as commanders of light armed companies in the regular regiments. The soldiers learned by training and taking active roles on expeditions with Rogers and his officers. Rogers also was ordered to write down his techniques which became known as his famous ranging rules. Of the approximately fifty-six cadets in that company, remaining records of about eighteen show some of the redcoat units involved. These records list three volunteers of the 4th Battalion of the 60th Regiment of Foot, two of the 2nd Battalion of the 60th Regiment of Foot, one of the 48th Regiment of Foot, one of the 55th Regiment of Foot, two of the 44th Regiment of Foot, two of the 22nd Regiment of Foot, three of the 42nd Regiment of Foot, and four listing no regiment. The cadets remained with Rogers throughout the campaign and were quartered with the other rangers on the island across from Fort Edward in December.[4]

In June, Eyre still commanded at Fort William Henry, and Lyman commanded at Fort Edward. There was a great mixture of provincial and redcoats that summer as the royal order of military rank had been rescinded. At Fort Edward and Fort William Henry, there were provincial regiments from Massachusetts, Connecticut, New York, New Hampshire, New Jersey, and Rhode Island. There were ranging companies from all the different colonies and two New York Independent companies. The British units consisted of the 27th, 35th, 42nd, 44th, 48th, 55th, and 60th Regiments of Foot, the 3rd Battalion of the Royal Artillery, and Royal Engineers. There were even sailors stationed at Fort William Henry. As was normal in the British and many provincial regiments, there was a good-sized enlistment of camp followers of both women and children with these garrisons. Johnson was only able to enlist a few Mohawks to scout for the army that year.

In July, the small groups of rangers were having problems penetrating the French advanced guard to acquire reconnaissance. Consequently, a detachment of three hundred and fifty Jersey Blues, as the New Jersey regiments were called, and a few New York militiamen, under Col. John Parker of New Jersey, were sent north in hope that the larger group could succeed. They proceeded north along the west side of Lake George in whaleboats. Near Sabbath Day Point, the enemy Indians, spotting the detachment, laid an ambush. Fire erupted from the bushes on shore, and a flotilla of Indian canoes cut off the possibility of retreat. Many of Parker's

---

[4] Burt G. Loescher, *The History of Rogers' Rangers: Officers and Non-Commissioned Officers*, 3 vols. (Burlingame, Ca.: Privately published by the author, 1957) 3; 81-84

detachment were shot in the initial engagement. When the men in the whaleboats tried to retreat, the Indians turned over many of the boats. Several men were also seen trying to surrender, and some leaped into the water hoping to escape. Many were captured and were horribly tortured before being killed. Three were eaten by the Indians on the spot. Of Parker's three hundred and fifty, three-quarters were tortured and killed.[5]

The remnants of Parker's Jersey Blues were warmly welcomed back to Fort William Henry's garrison where the rest of his regiment had remained. Eyre's garrison now had been replaced by five companies of the 35th Regiment of Foot and two ranger companies under the command of Lt. Col. George Monro of the 35th. Putnam and forty of his men were sent out toward the French forts. The rangers ran into several canoes and turned around telling Monro they had seen a French flotilla. Monro ordered most of his garrison to move to the spot that Johnson's army had defended in 1755 and ordered a breastwork to be built around that camp.

Back at Fort Edward, Webb, commander of the fort and expedition, sent a letter calling up the New York militia and urged the other colonies to send reinforcements, believing the French were on their way to attack. Webb sent Monro a reinforcement of Col. Joseph Frye's Massachusetts regiment, some Massachusetts artificers, about a dozen ships' carpenters of Col. Jonathan Bagley's Massachusetts regiment, and a detachment of the 60th Regiment of Foot. That gave Monro a garrison of units of the 27th, 35th, and 60th Regiments of Foot, Royal Artillery, several engineers, sailors, and provincials from Massachusetts, New York, New Hampshire, New Jersey, Rhode Island, and two companies of New Independents. Monro's largest contingent was from Massachusetts.

---

[5] Francis Parkman, *Montcalm and Wolfe* (New York: Atheneum, 1984), 282. Timothy J. Todish, *America's First World War* (Grand Rapids, MI: Suagothel Productions, Ltd., 1982), 36-37.

THE SIEGE OF FORT WILLIAM HENRY. On August 2, four whaleboats from the Fort William Henry garrison were attacked, and, two hours later, a French fleet under command of the Marquis de Montcalm appeared in full view of the fort. Montcalm's Indians and Canadians started to encircle the fort and the entrenched camp while he ordered the digging of trenches in which to place his artillery to lay siege. Monro ordered three hundred Massachusetts soldiers to sally out and attempt to secure the military road leading to Fort Edward. They were driven back with heavy losses. By that time, there were nearly two thousand men in the entrenched camp. For four days, the Indians continually harassed the entrenched camp while Montcalm's trenches were dug on the west side of the fort. On the fifth day of the siege, William Johnson arrived at Fort Edward with 1,500 New York militiamen and 180 Indians. When Webb refused to allow them to reinforce Fort William Henry, the Indians stripped off their clothes and threw them at Webb's feet in a gesture of disgust.

Then, on day six, the French artillery began to bombard. Monro and Webb had been able to somehow keep sporadic communications between the two forts via runners through these early days of the siege. Then, a message from Webb urging Monro to look for terms of surrender was captured by Montcalm's Indians. That allowed Montcalm the knowledge that reinforcements were not forthcoming.

On August eighth, the French artillery had been advanced to 250 yards from the fort. At that range, the exploding shells were killing and wounding many in the fort. The fort itself was holding up quite well against the cannonade. Then, on August ninth, the enemy artillery was only 150 yards away from the fort. Monro called a council of war, and at 6 A.M. a flag of truce was raised over Fort William Henry. Negotiators met from both sides, and Montcalm offered Monro and his garrison the honors of war.

The next morning, they were to march out with drums beating and colours flying. Soldiers and officers were to retain their arms and baggage. One cannon was allowed to escort the column. The French were to provide an escort to take the column to Fort Edward. This was in exchange for an oath not to serve against the French or their allies for eighteen months, and all French, Canadian, and Indian prisoners taken in America were to be released at Fort Carillon within three months.

Monro accepted the terms of surrender and moved his garrison into the entrenched camp except for those too sick or wounded to move. The Indians attacked and killed some of these invalids upon the leaving of Monro's troops. Around midnight, the English garrison tried to start for Fort Edward but were forced back into the entrenchments.

After spending another night with no sleep, Monro and his men headed out at 5 A.M. As the first regiments of regulars left the camp, the Indians, who had collected around them, intimidated the officers and men to give up haversacks, knapsacks, and clothing. At the rear of the column, the camp followers were being pulled out of the ranks and taken into the woods, some being killed in front of the men. Monro complained, to no avail, and the column moved forward, becoming frantic. The redcoats began to break and run into the woods and down the road toward Fort Edward. As the provincials left the camp, the same treatment occurred. Indians also were pulling blacks, Indians, and mulattos from the ranks and hustling them away. Frye, leading the Yankee advance down the road, could hold them together no longer and joined his men as they began to sprint into the woods and down the road.

As the Fort William Henry garrison started arriving at Fort Edward within hours, panic started at Fort Edward. Many men, arriving in only their shirts, told terrifying eyewitness accounts of killings and scalpings. Webb immediately sent couriers to the Governors requesting reinforcement. Within five days, there were over four thousand militia at Fort Edward. By that time, the threat of Montcalm advancing to Fort Edward was gone as he had burned Fort William Henry and had fallen back to Fort Carillon. Ultimately, the colonial militias were sent straight back to their homes to prepare defenses against their frontiers.

As the autumn fell on upper New York, the French were reveling in victory. At Fort Edward, there were still soldiers and followers dribbling in from the sprint or capture from Fort William Henry. This was to be one of the worst disasters in North America for the British army. Fort William Henry had withstood cannonading, but, without reinforcement, her garrison could not. Montcalm's failure to stop the Indian massacre on the surrendered garrison would be told at Yankee hearths for generations. The garrison was maintained at Fort Edward, now the only English fort between the French and Albany. Connecticut, not in the Fort William Henry garrison during the massacre, even ordered three companies to remain at Fort Edward that winter as rangers.

THE CAMPAIGN OF 1758

Some of the men who comprised the winter garrison at Fort Edward were Dunn's Rangers, Rogers' Rangers, and several bateaux men.   In January, Lord Loudon ordered Rogers to raise four new companies for his independent corps. The four companies were to be recruited from New England. Rogers' Mohican Indian companies were increased to one hundred men each, and a fifty-man company of Connecticut Mohegans was placed with his rangers.   By March, Rogers' companies were complete and at Fort Edward.

THE BATTLE ON SNOWSHOES. Col. William Haviland, of the 60th Regiment of Foot and commander of Fort Edward, ordered Rogers out in March on a scout towards Fort Carillon with 180 rangers and volunteers. They rowed up Lake George in the cloak of darkness; landing, they left the lake, and skirted the back of the western mountains, heading within a few miles of the French fort.   On March thirteenth, Rogers' forward guard reported an enemy party heading up the frozen stream (Trout Brook) near the rangers' flank.   Rogers faced his detachment toward the brook, and when the enemy appeared, they fired, killing some, and the rest fell back as about half of Rogers' men pursued them. Unbeknownst to Rogers, this was only an advanced party, and now in hot pursuit, his men ran head on into the French and Indian main body.

In the erupting fire, about fifty of Rogers' men were killed. The remainder fell back, and Rogers formed his men on a ridge and fought off the enemy attacks, many times firing with only yards between the opponents. Eight officers and one hundred men lay dead. This fight continued till dusk; then the survivors dispersed and fled. Rogers and about twenty men retreated up a large mountain (Rogers' Rock) to the east near Lake George under pursuit of the enemy. A running battle occurred up the slopes with more losses.   Finally, making their escape, the remnants of the detachment reached Fort Edward two days later. In April, Rogers was commissioned a major by General Abercrombie.

Changes took place in the redcoat regiments between 1757 and 1758. They augmented their units to encompass not just grenadier and hat companies, but a light infantry company as well. The men were issued lighter clothing and equipment which was adapted for forest warfare. There were also several new regiments raised specifically as light or ranger regiments. Some of these included the first Battalion of the 60th, Lord Howe's 55th, and Thomas Gage's 80th Regiment of Foot. These units were to emulate American rangers. The units and companies of light infantry were formed because of unreliability and insubordination problems with ranger units. It was hoped that these problems would be solved by disbanding the ranger units and replacing them with regular light units commanded by regular British officers.

Spring was bringing together the largest and most diverse British army to Lake George to date, nearly fifteen thousand. Of the nine thousand provincials, there were regiments from Massachusetts, Connecticut, New Jersey, New York, New Hampshire, and Rhode Island. New Jersey also had a company of one hundred colonial grenadiers. Rangers consisted of Partridge's, Dunn's, Putnam's, and Rogers' Rangers. Wagoners and bateaux men transported men and gear, and fought with the rest of the army. The six thousand redcoats consisted of the 27th, 42nd, 44th, 46th, 55th, 60th, and 80th Regiments of Foot, along with detachments of Royal Artillery and Royal Engineers. That year, there were not just engineers listed but their assistants were as well. Some of their assistants were Lieutenants Clerk, Garth, Meyer, Ratzer, and Mr. Rivet and Mr. Psister. Following these regiments were auxiliary troops, sutlers, and camp followers.

Each regiment of one thousand men was issued eight wagons. Regiments of seven hundred men were given six wagons to move baggage and stores. Ox carts transported provisions. Fortifications were being built as depots between Fort Edward and Lake George. Half Way Brook Post (half way between Fort Edward and Old Fort William Henry) had a picketed fort built and in June, a fort had been built east of the swamp near the ruins of Fort William Henry.

The British command recommended that women and children not follow their regiments as they advanced to Fort Carillon. Consequently, they were left at Fort Edward and Lake George camps. A list was to be compiled of women of the regiments; four were allowed per company in regiments of one thousand men, and three were allowed per company in regiments of seven hundred men. The regiments were to list women to be victualed, and those to serve as nurses in the general hospital. An order was given that any woman who refused to serve in the hospital would be drummed out of camp and given no provisions. Even Lord Howe brought his mistress, the Baroness Kielmansegge.

ABERCROMBIE ATTACKS FORT CARILLON. By July 5, the grand army under Gen. James Abercrombie and his second in command, Lord Howe of the 55th Regiment of Foot, loaded a thousand boats with their supplies and artillery and advanced up Lake George. The flotilla had the 80th and 55th Regiments of Foot and Rogers in the advance in whaleboats followed by Bradstreet and his bateaux men. The main body of the army followed in three columns. The center column consisted of the redcoats followed by two floating batteries. The flanking columns were composed of the Massachusetts and New Jersey Regiments on the right, the Connecticut Regiments on the left, followed by baggage, supplies, and artillery. The rear of the flotilla was covered by Partridge's Royal Hunters (rangers, or light infantry) and the Royal Artillery.

DEATH OF LORD HOWE. On the sixth, around 10 A.M., the army landed at a cove near Fort Carillon. By noon the entire army was on shore. Then, advancing in three columns, Lord

Howe went forward of the center with Putnam and his rangers. Both the British and French advanced guard seemed to get disoriented in the wooded terrain. Lord Howe advanced forward with the hope of driving the French off the field with his light troops. The two adversaries engaged, and one of the first shots hit Howe in the chest, killing him. Putnam took command of the advance, and the columns continued to push forward. Bagley, on the right, was ordered to push the French flank, and the British subdued the enemy.

Howe's death was tragic to the men, both provincial and redcoat. He was well-liked, personable, and esteemed by all. Another tragedy to the expedition was that Howe no longer was to be able to check Abercrombie's command. The army returned to the landing, and a detachment was sent forward to secure the ground toward Fort Carillon. The area was secured. On July eighth, Abercrombie's army formed for attack.

The French had remained in advance of their fort and had taken the last two days to fell trees away from the fort, forming a natural abatis. To make it more difficult, ends of the branches had been sharpened. Then, the French ordered an earth and log breastwork built to fire from behind. This obstacle course would prove devastating to Abercrombie's army.

Early that day, Johnson arrived at Carillon with 300 Mohawks and Oneidas, and Captain Jacob (Cheeksaunkun) arrived with 140 Mohicans. They climbed a mountain across the water from the fort and fired from afar all day. The British sent forward the rangers, light infantry, and bateaux men and formed an advanced skirmish line as the provincials formed by regiments from one end of the breastwork to the other. At that time, Abercrombie should have advanced his artillery but never did. For some unknown reason, he wished to carry the breastwork by bayonet. The provincials now began advancing and firing from the edge of the woods. Then, in three columns, the redcoats advanced though the intervals between the provincials, leaving the Connecticut and New Jersey regiments in reserve as a rear guard.

The redcoats advanced and fired to no avail for about an hour. Then, Abercrombie ordered another advance on the abatis and breastwork. The columns could not hold together through the abatis in order to concentrate an assault after breaching the area between abatis and breastwork. The redcoats were ordered time and time again to advance and take the works, each time being cut to pieces by small arms fire and grape shot from French cannons. Then, at 5 P.M., two columns combined for an assault on the right flank. At one fleeting moment, an officer and a handful of men of the 42nd Highlanders jumped into the French works, infiltrating their lines, to be bayoneted immediately. After the final attempt, the army fell back with the rangers, and some provincials sporadically gave covering fire from the woods. The next morning, the British army left in such a hurry and confusion that they left many shoes that had been sucked off their feet in the mud and great amounts of supplies and provisions. Frantically, devastated and forlorned, Abercrombie's army scurried back to their picketed forts and Lake George.

With this disappointed and frightened army, the British needed to prepare for a French retort, and ordered their men to start building a picketed fort. On July 12, they started a new fort about one hundred rods east of the other fort built in June near Old Fort William Henry. Soldiers were also busied destroying Montcalm's works from his siege of Fort William Henry in 1757. They also were digging stumps for tented camps and building boats, blockhouses, storehouses, hospitals, and barracks. Captain Loring of the Royal Navy was in charge of constructing boats with his sailors, carpenters, and with help from bateaux men and provincial troops. Most of the rangers and light infantry units were scouring the countryside for advanced parties of an enemy attack. The hospitals at Fort Edward and Lake George were not just kept busy with casualties from the battle but also from the multitude of soldiers who became ill from the unsanitary conditions in the camps. There were also large numbers of men suffering from physical symptoms caused by mental anguish from their experiences in battle.

THE CAMPAIGN OF 1759

Gen. Jeffrey Amherst led the British advance of 1759 up the Lake George–Lake Champlain Corridor. He started accumulating his army at Fort Edward and Lake George. Fort Edward by that year had become the largest group of buildings in British North America north of Albany. Amherst's provincials consisted of men from Massachusetts, Connecticut, Rhode Island, New York, New Hampshire, and New Jersey. Bateaux men and wagoners were organized under officers into companies of fifty men.

For the regulars, Amherst gave orders that all the regiments were to form the most active men into light infantry companies. In addition to these companies, Amherst's had troops from the 1st, 17th, 22nd, 27th, 42nd, 47th, 55th, 60th, 77th, and 80th Regiments of Foot. The army was also composed of rangers, Royal Artillery, Royal Engineers, Royal Navy, auxiliary, sutlers, and followers. Indians from the Mohawk, Oneida, Mohegan (from Connecticut) and Mohican (from Massachusetts) tribes assisted Amherst's army. These natives were usually within companies of twenty-five or thirty, to one hundred men. In February, Rogers raised another company of Indians for his corps. These may have been Mohawks, giving him three different tribes within his regiment (Mohican, Mohegan and Mohawk).

As this army moved up to Lake George, Amherst kept his troops extremely busy building new forts. Fort Edward was a huge complex, and now as they moved forward up the military road, Amherst ordered a fort built every three to four miles. Four miles north from Fort Edward, the army built the first stockaded outpost, Four Mile Post (see Map 2). Then, on the Fort Edward side (south) of Half Way Brook, they built Fort Amherst. That gave the army two forts at this spot and a stockaded garrison ground. Between these forts and Lake

George, the army constructed Fort William. At Lake George, the army was busied by constructing a stockaded area, a fortified blockhouse named Fort Gage, and a fort that never was finished, named Fort George. Captain Loring of the Royal Navy was building on Lake George again. He was in charge of the construction of a fourteen-gun sloop.

On July 21, Amherst's 5,743 redcoats and like number of provincials launched their flotilla and set out to attack Fort Carillon. The army arrived with no opposition, making it to the French breastworks of 1758. At that point, Amherst ordered artillery trenching to begin. The Fort Carillon garrison began a bombardment of Amherst's trenching. Realizing the fort would indeed fall to this British army, all but a four-hundred-man French rear guard retreated to Fort St. Frédéric. The four hundred Frenchmen put up a good cannonade. Amherst ordered his own men not to return fire until all his cannons were in place. When the British guns were six hundred yards out, the four hundred Frenchmen also deserted the fort, setting fire to the wooden parts of the fort and starting a match to blow up the powder magazine. When the fort blew up, only one bastion was damaged, and the wooden parts were gone. Instead of pursuing the French, Amherst had his men rebuild this fort, which would be renamed Fort Ticonderoga. A few days later, he received information from his scouts that the French had also retreated and left Fort St. Frédéric. Amherst advanced part of his army and took the area, building a new fort, Crown Point, with multiple exterior fortified redouts.

Early in August under Amherst's orders, more building was done. In order to dominate Lake Champlain, the British needed a superior fleet. Under Captain Loring's supervision, two radows mounting six twelve-pounders and a twenty-four-pounder in their bow, four row galleys carrying eighteen-pounders in their bow, one flat boat with six-pounders, four bay boats with swivel guns, a brig, and finally an armed sloop were built. This would be superior to the four French boats on the lake, and Amherst's army would be able to proceed up the lake, safely following the retreating French army. Proving superiority on Lake Champlain, Amherst advanced up the lake, but by that time it was late fall, and weather halted his advancement into the heart of French Canada where the other British armies also were successful in their campaigns.

THE CAMPAIGN OF 1760

Like all of the previous campaigns, the British army in 1760 had several different directions to send armies. The army heading north up the all-important corridor was led by Gen. William Haviland. For his thrust north, Haviland was followed by soldiers of the 1st, 17th, 27th, 42nd, 77th, and 80th Regiments of Foot, Royal Artillery, Royal Engineers, along with the light infantries. The colonial regiments in 1760 were from Massachusetts, Connecticut, New York, New Hampshire, Rhode Island, New Jersey, New York Independents, ranger units, and Native Americans.

Regiments of one thousand men were issued three ox carts for sutlers, and regiments of seven hundred men were issued two ox carts or when proceeding by water were given two small bateaux. Regiments of one thousand also were allowed three wagons for every two companies for baggage. When water travel was employed, they were issued a like number of bateaux. Each commanding officer was given one wagon or bateau for baggage. His staff also had one or the other.

Orders were given for no women to follow the regiments, but there were many references to followers in the corridor. In the Massachusetts regiments, each company was allowed four women, or four pence in lieu of each woman's provisions. In June, a great number of followers were recorded passing Ticonderoga on their way from Crown Point to Albany. Also, no women or sutlers were to leave Crown Point without written permission.

When leaving Crown Point and heading north on Lake Champlain, Haviland's army consisted of around 4,400 redcoats, provincials, rangers, and Indians. They advanced, capturing the French fleet and several forts as the enemy employed desertion of fort, retreat, and stand tactics. By August, Haviland's army was close to Quebec and the merging of the British armies. By September ninth, the fighting in North America was over. The French had surrendered and only the clean up of small western outposts was needed.

Part II:

Clothing, Gear and Equipment: Issuance and Descriptions

The basic clothing, gear, and equipment of French and Indian War soldiers were quite basic in design and style, no matter if redcoat or provincial.

FOOTWEAR. The shoes worn by eighteenth-century soldiers were generally round-toed, low-heeled shoes. The usual closure was a brass buckle at the vamp with varying lengths of tongue. Officers, affording the extra cost, wore better quality shoes, and many purchased more ornate shoes, often with silver or gold buckles. Those of the provincial regiments also may have worn unissued shoes, similar, but with lace or ribbon closures. Officers in many regiments, especially the regulars, were ordered to wear boots when the men wore marching gaiters. These were full-calved, straight-cut boots with cuffs similar to today's riding boots. The leather used was almost always black in the military and had an almost suede texture, only appearing smooth after wear. Moccasins or Indian shoes were also worn by many rangers, provincials, light infantry and civilian auxiliaries as makeshift footwear when shoes had worn out. Of course, this was the primary footwear of all natives. The majority of moccasins were center-seamed, popular in the eastern woodland tribes, and usually made of moose or elk hide.

HOSE OR SOCKS were knee length or longer. Most issued soldier's hose were woolen and varied by the regiment within the regulars. Hose could vary widely from one man to the other in the provincial regiments. In general, the most standard hose worn in the British army was light to medium grey and

white to off-white ribbed hose. Officers could vary their hose
in texture, color, and fabric. Some gentlemen officers wore
clocked cotton or linen hose, some woolen. Colors varied
greatly, but generally were white, off-white, or grey in the
officer corps. Highland troops were issued woolen hose
woven into fabric, cut out in the shape of the leg and sewn up
the back of the calf. Most of these hose were red and white
woven into diamond patterns (a harlequin design). Sometimes
extra tartan also was fashioned into hose.

GAITERS. Over the hose, most soldiers wore canvas gaiters
(spatterdashes). These were heavy linen canvas tubes cut to fit
the leg trimly. Gaiters were cut to reach half way up the thigh
and reached to within one-half to one inch from the sole of the
shoe. The outside of the gaiter was closed by twenty-five to
thirty black horn buttons on each. Gaiters were equipped with
a strap that reached under the shoes at the arch and at the top
of the calf, just below the knee. They were held up by a black
leather set of buckled garters. There was also attached to the
front, a canvas cap sewn over the instep of the shoes to keep
moisture and debris from falling into the shoe. Provincial
regiments, if issued gaiters, were probably just issued one pair.
Regulars, on the other hand, were issued two pair. White
gaiters were issued for dress and parade, and brown, and in
later war black, gaiters were issued for fatigue and marching
duties (see Appendix 1).

LEGGINGS. Rangers, some provincials, Indians, some light
infantry, and a few redcoat units wore or were issued leggings
(leggins, leggers, leggens). These were also made when gaiters
wore out or for extra warmth. Leggings usually were woolen
fabric wrapped around the lower three-quarters of the leg and
tied around the leg or held up with garters. Many were also a
tube of wool sewn with the seam in the front, leaving it open
several inches at the foot, allowing them to rest slightly open
on the instep of the foot. A few issued leggings also may have

had the toe cap, as on gaiters. Another common leggins material used by Indians and rangers was deerskin.

BREECHES. Most soldiers were issued woolen breeches (britches). Breeches were knee-length pants with a tall waistband, and were fastened by bands at the knee. Buttons and buckles were both used for knee fasteners. Breeches fastened with a gusset and laced in the back of the waistband. They were baggy in the seat and used two different fly closures. The most common military fly was a single row of buttons called the French fly. Some men purchased or were issued drop-front breeches. To coordinate with the 1751 Uniform Warrant, soldiers with blue facings (cuffs, lapels, and linings) were issued blue wool breeches. All other units were issued red. This held true for most redcoat regiments. Provincial units, who were issued breeches, usually wore red. Some regiments, as well as ranger units, and quite a few men who purchased their own breeches, had wool, linen, canvas linen, and leather, which was quite popular.

TROUSERS were rarer in the military, but a few regiments were issued canvas trousers. These were made the same as breeches but had a full leg and were long. Another form of trouser, common among sailors and maritime workers, were slops. Slops were again made like breeches but had a very full leg without a knee band. These varied in length from the knee to the ankle. Most were made of canvas linen in its natural color, but some were colors, and many were striped linen. Trousers and slops were also very popular as workman's pants and were commonly worn as overalls to protect other clothing.

SHIRTS. The shirt of the Seven Years' War soldier was a large garment made from rectangles and gussets. Most military shirts were made of bleached or unbleached linen in white to off-white color. Many regiments also issued checked linen in blue or black for work and fatigue. Some regiments also issued coarse, canvas linen work shirts or smocks. These were usually natural color. The work shirts were common for workmen in civilian life, and farmers and woodsmen also preferred them. All three of these types of shirts were large in the body and very full in the sleeve. Both the collar and cuff were quite narrow and used either a button or cufflink for closure. Shirts were made long, half way down the thigh, as they were shirt, nightshirt, and undershirt all in one. Some regiments or companies of regiments were issued shirts with a ruffled cuff and neck opening. Most officers wore ruffled shirts of very fine linen.

CRAVATS, STOCKS AND NECK SCARVES. Soldiers wore the same shirts for several days at a time, and both for style and to keep the appearance of a clean shirt, men were issued and purchased coverings for around the neck. There were various garments used by the British regiments. The cravat and stock were the most popular. The cravat was simply a rectangular piece of linen folded and looped around the neck and folded over once through itself in front, similar to a modern tie. The stock was a piece of linen with leather tabs sewn to each end. The linen was wrapped around the front of the neck over the collar and fastened at the back of the neck by either a buckle or lace. The linen of the stock was usually white or black. The other neck covering used by soldiers was a simple neck scarf. These were purchased items. They varied from silk to linen and were available in many different colors.

WAISTCOATS. The waistcoat was a garment issued to all uniformed soldiers of the eighteenth century. This was similar to our vests of today. Waistcoats, along with the breeches, were called the small clothes. As were the breeches, the waistcoat was made of wool. All redcoat units were issued red waistcoats. Provincial units were usually issued red but some received blue. Rangers' and purchased waistcoats worn by non-uniformed units varied in color and fabric (see Appendix 2). The length was usually mid-thigh and straight cut on the hem. The waistcoat was closed by a series of buttons from the neck to the waist. Regiments with regimental lace usually had laced waistcoats (see Appendices 3 and 4). Officers usually had the same color waistcoats as their men but laced theirs, depending on the regiment, with gold or silver braid (see Appendix 5).

REGIMENTALS, or uniform coats, were the primary issued garment of the army. These were wool coats with lapels and cuffs. They were wool-lined and laced in the regimental lace of the unit. The cut of the lapel and cuff varied, but were uniform within each regiment according to the 1751 Uniform Warrant. On the left shoulder was stitched a wool tab that buttoned over the cartridge box strap. The length of the coat was mid-thigh and was made to hook back at the skirts for parade. The body of the regular's coat was red, and the facings and linings were regulated by regiment (see Appendix 6). Many regiments had a brick-type red, commonly called madder red, that is duller than scarlet. Provincial coats were of the same style as regulars, but colors varied according to the colony's preference. There was a conscious push to uniform the provincials in blue coats with red facings. Many ranger and light infantry units' coats were similar but made or cut into a shorter length. The Highland regimental was a shorter coat, made with cuffs but no lapel, until late war. Highland coats were made with round collars of facing colors. Pockets of all regimentals were made to be functional, and were usually very large and deep in design, to carry extra food and gear.

OFFICERS of all regiments, with few exceptions, laced their regimentals with gold or silver braid according to regimental warrants. Scarlet was the common officers' wool. Many officers also distinguished themselves by attaching silver or gold aguillettes (loops of braid or ribbon similar to modern shoulder loops) on the shoulder. They also wore a gold or silver gorget; a metal crescent worn around the neck as a badge of rank. The majority of these had the royal crest embossed or engraved on them. The gorget was hung around the neck by a ribbon of the regiment's facing color. Many officers had a ribbon rosette or metal button at the ends of the ribbon to attach the gorget to the ribbon. Another badge of rank worn over the right shoulder, except for Highland officers who wore theirs over the left because of their sword, was a crimson silk sash. Many of these sashes were made of loosely woven silk mesh. A few were made of water-stained silk. Most officers also carried swords with gold or silver hilts, with a sword knot of crimson and gold or silver woven together. The sword knot was a tasseled loop in which the soldier could insert his hand. If he dropped his sword in battle, he would not lose it altogether and could easily retrieve it.

NON-COMMISSIONED OFFICERS, sergeants, and corporals also had distinctions. Sergeants had coats similar to the enlisted men, possibly more scarlet, but in the early war, a few regiments were still lacing sergeant's uniforms in silver. All sergeants wore a worsted wool sash around their waist. This sash was to be scarlet with a stripe of facing color down the middle. Those regiments with red facings were to have a stripe of white. Corporals' coats were identical to the soldiers'. Their only distinction was a white worsted shoulder knot worn on the shoulder strap of the coat. The only variance of this was that the Massachusetts regiments wore yellow shoulder knots in later years of the war.

SOLDIERS' HATS. A soldier's hat was the tricorn. This was a black, fur-felted, round brimmed hat blank that was turned up on three sides, forming a three-cornered or three-sided hat. The tricorn was laced up on the sides by white worsted cord and was trimmed with white worsted tape, called ferreting. On the left side of the hat, a black cockade of silk ribbon was placed under the white cording and held in place by a regimental button.

BUTTONS. The majority of buttons on soldiers' uniforms, especially early in the war, were plain, domed, and pewter with a shanked back. There is evidence of this from buttons retrieved from a vessel which sank while sailing to America in the late war. Buttons found on this vessel were numbered, regimental buttons. It is possible that regiments were starting to implement these new buttons which show up on a uniform warrant shortly after the war. Officers' buttons seem to have been up to the individual, but there is a lot of evidence of a gold button with a basket weave pattern being popular with officers.

FORAGE CAPS. The forage cap was the other issued hat worn by the soldiers. These were made from scraps of old uniforms. Forage caps were red wool turned up, with a piece of wool the same color as the uniform facing. They were lined with coarse linen. The hat was shaped like a night cap, which hung to the side of the head. The cut of the facing color varied to about four inches. The top of the forage cap was usually finished off with a white, worsted tassel. These originated as caps used to collect foraged food. Soldiers were to wear forage caps for night duty and fatigue duty.

WATCH COATS were also issued to the regiments. These were issued for guard duty. There were only enough of these issued for the guards, and many soldiers purchased or made their own coats for cold weather. Watch coats were great coats, to be worn over regimental clothing. They were made full, with a large cape in order to cover the head, and with an under cape. Most were made of blanket-weight blue wool. These coats were single-breasted and fastened shut with a single row of buttons. They were made to hang below the calf. Many men, making their own, could simply fashion a coat out of blankets. These were undoubtedly mainly made from white issued, British military blankets. They were made of rectangles and fastened in the front by wool tape, buttons, or a sash.

COLD WEATHER ITEMS. Other cold weather items used were usually made or purchased by the men unless they were part of a winter garrison. Then, colonels would have them made and paid for by the soldiers. Mittens, gloves, scarves, wool leggins, and even wool-lined, oversized moccasins were common cold weather gear.

RAIN GEAR was not issued but was used by some soldiers. Oilcloth was very common. All regiments had tarps of oilcloth to cover equipment. Most soldiers were familiar with oilcloth at home, and many made, brought, or purchased oilcloth from sutlers. A piece of oilcloth could easily be wrapped around a soldier's shoulders, or a hole could be sliced in the center and slipped over the head. Oilcloth, though very flammable, was ample protection from rain. Sailors and maritime workers, of which there were many in the provincial ranks, were used to wearing jackets made of oilcloth. It makes good sense then, that these jackets were common with men who had them (see Fig. 3).

ISSUANCE. For the issue of clothing, the colonel of the regiment was to furnish his men with items, withhold the cost from their pay, and petition the crown for additional costs and repayment. Every regiment had civilian clothiers, those for the redcoats were primarily in England; provincial and other units had clothiers here in America. These clothiers developed patterns based on the 1751 Uniform Warrant. This pattern then was sent to the general officers for their agreement on conformance to the warrants. When accepted, the pattern was sent to the colonel of the regiment. At this point, the colonel ordered a uniform to be made by the clothier.

TAILORING. First, the fabric was washed and pre-shrunk. Then a man from the regiment was chosen to be a "pattern man." The clothier made a uniform which was tailored to fit the pattern man. When the uniform was completed, the pattern man was sent back to the regiment to display it to the colonel for final approval. The uniform was then sent to the clothier, and the colonel's order for uniforms for his regiment

Fig. 3. These men are dressed for inclement weather. Some of the clothes are issued items, others are adaptations made by the individual soldier. The three men on the left are clothed in wool, ranging from left to right; a blanket wrapped around the shoulders, great coat, and blanket coat. The soldier on the right is wearing a piece of oilskin. He has taken an oilskin tarp and cut a slit in the center. By opening the tarp he can wear it as a poncho to keep out the rain.

was made and shipped unlined in barrels, crates, and bundles. Clothiers made these uniforms in small, medium, and large. They were unlined for ease of tailoring and cost of shipping. Upon arrival at the regiment, tailors were recruited from the ranks of men who were skilled in the trade in civilian life. These men, under the care of a regimental tailor, took the measurements of the soldiers and began their work. The tailors adjusted and lined the uniforms at that time. The woolen uniforms were made of kersey, a twill weave, and cheap woolen broadcloth. Lining was made from shalloon or serge, a middle-weight, inexpensive, hard-wearing wool. The waistcoat was also made of kersey. Some regimental coats were saved after their year of service and were worn as a utility coat or re-cut into waistcoats to save money. Breeches were made of kersey, as well, but lined in linen.

After tailoring was complete, the soldiers received a final fitting, and then the uniform was inspected one last time to ensure it matched the pattern man's uniform. If a coat was found to be too small at this point, gussets were commonly added. Now complete, the uniform was issued. This process usually started with the grenadier company, and then continued in alphabetical order (company A, B, C . . .). After the clothier was finished, the tailors were done, and the uniforms were issued, the pattern was returned to the colonel where it remained until uniforms were to be issued early the next year.

GEAR AND EQUIPMENT. Every soldier of the corridor was issued, in some form or another, a haversack, canteen, cartridge box, belt and frog, sword or belt axe, musket, bayonet, knapsack, blanket, tent, camp axe, cooking kettle, equipment to take care of gear, and equipment to take care of their musket. The haversack was a coarse, natural-colored linen bag used by the soldier to carry his provisions.

CANTEENS varied from kidney-shaped tin flasks to provincial issues of round, single or double-banded canteens of wood (wooden bottles), barrel-shaped wood canteens, leather-covered glass bottles, and gourds.

AMMUNITION BAGS AND BOXES. At the beginning of the war, many units were issued a powder horn and bullet pouch. This practice continued throughout the war, but there were increasing numbers of cartridge boxes substituted. Bullet pouches varied in texture, style, and color, with next to no contemporary military descriptions. They were usually open leather bags with flap closures, worn over the shoulder. They carried musket balls and items needed to clean and fire the musket. It is also possible that the term bullet pouch was synonymous with cartridge box. The cartridge box was also a bag worn over the left shoulder, hanging on the right hip. These were quite standard. Most were black leather with an interior and larger exterior flap to keep out moisture. Inside was a wooden block with rows of drilled holes to hold pre-made paper cartridges. Straps were usually of a tan/buff color leather, and, if British issue, had three double D issued brass buckles. Some units such as grenadiers were also issued a belly box. This was an additional cartridge box worn in the front of the body on a belt around the waist. It normally consisted of a wooden block like the shoulder style but was smaller and had a black leather flap for moisture protection.

BELTS FOR HOLDING WEAPONS. Some sort of belt was needed to hold edged weapons. Usually, this was a tan/buff colored waist belt with a frog (leather carriage) on the left side. Within the belt frog (belt and hanger), the soldier carried either his issued sword (usually a saber) or a small belt axe. As woodland warfare increased in the corridor, the swords were increasingly replaced with the axe. Also held in the frog was the bayonet. This was a socket-style, long, pointed bayonet. There were three sides on issued bayonets, with two sides being concave. The majority of soldiers receiving Brown Bess muskets received bayonets. All of these edged weapons were cased in leather scabbards that were usually black.

MUSKETS. The standard issued musket was a seventy-five caliber, smoothbore military musket called the "Brown Bess." These usually had a forty-six inch barrel. These flintlocks were equipped with a tan/buff sling which was attached to the stock with swivels. It was common for soldiers to be issued sixty-nine caliber musket balls for ease of loading with paper cartridges. Another common practice was to cut the barrels, shortening the musket for ease of movement in the woods. There is also evidence of smaller caliber carbines being issued to some regiments. Some light troops were also issued French muskets, probably captured arms. In 1758 and 1759, each company was issued rifles, ten for each unit. In the provincial regiments, it was common for the colonies to offer bounties if men brought their own firelocks that could pass inspection. Colonies also impressed arms for their troops. There were also years when the colonial troops were primarily issued King's Arms (Brown Bess muskets). Consequently, colonial soldiers carried a variety of firelocks. An officer, when carrying a musket, was armed normally with a fuzil or fuzee. These were small caliber muskets of a slightly smaller stature, built to emulate the Brown Bess.

KNAPSACKS, SNAPSACKS AND PACKS. In order to carry personal belongings and extra clothes, soldiers were issued knapsacks, snapsacks, or packs. The most common knapsack was a hair-on leather bag with an outer flap worn over the right shoulder. These were worn hanging on the back towards the left side by a tan/buff leather strap. The bag usually was linen-lined and closed with three straps and buckles in front. Some had compartments inside, and some were closed by buttons. Cow, horse, or goat hide of a brown color were the standard issue. Some knapsacks were similar but of a linen canvas. Some may have been similar to two pockets or haversacks sewn together at the top and strapped together at the bottom.

The snapsack was a tube sewn shut at one end and tied shut at the other end. These were slung over the shoulder like the knapsack. Most snapsacks were also hair-on leather, but some were leather or linen canvas. The snapsack was not as popular as the knapsack in this war.

The pack was a canvas, leather, or hair-on bag which was slung over both shoulders on straps. Packs were closed by straps or buttons. They had single and multiple compartments. Historians do not know how many packs like these were issued or if the term pack may have been synonymous with knapsack.

Regulars and most provincial troops were issued knapsacks or packs of some form. Provincial troops, rangers, and Indians were not as uniform with their issue. Consequently, there was a lot of variability. Many of these troops wore non-uniformed packs.

BLANKETS were an issued item to the majority of troops. The standard issued British blanket was a heavy, white wool blanket. Many of these blankets had several thin blue or black stripes on them. Many of the provincial soldiers were also issued these blankets from the King's stores. It was common for colonies to impress blankets, or to pay a bounty to soldiers who brought or purchased their own blankets. Because of the variables, many men had non-white blankets. Soldiers' blankets were usually rolled and held under the flap of the knapsack, or were also rolled and carried over the shoulder on a strap called a tumpline. Many were folded lengthwise and carried diagonally over the shoulder and across the body like a bandoleer.

TENTS. Men were divided into messes (five or six men) to share equipment and for provisioning. The tents issued to the soldiers were made of heavy, white, linen canvas. The typical soldier's tent was a wedge tent and was issued to every mess. The wedge tents had two upright poles, one ridge pole, and thirteen pegs (stakes). The dimensions were six feet wide, by seven feet long, by six feet high. It appears that a common practice of the soldiers was to cover the dirt floor of the tent with bark. Some units were also issued wedge tents with a bell-shaped back. This was originally a dragoon tent made with room in the bell for horse equipment. Some larger wedge tents were also used. These nine by nine foot, seven foot-six inch high tents were probably for the use of non-commissioned officers. There were also very large "bell-backs" for artillery.

Officers were issued marquees, wall tents, and wedge tents. The walls on the marquee were taller than the usual wall tents; about four feet. Marquees usually had only three poles with ropes strung out in all directions to stretch the canvas. Marquees were to be scalloped around the top, with worsted tape in the facing color of the regiment. Captains were issued an eight to ten foot wide by twelve to fourteen foot long marquee with a six foot ridge pole, and which stood eight feet high. Subalterns (lieutenants and ensigns) were issued an eight foot by ten foot tent with a four foot ridge pole, for every two officers.

Wall tents were popular, especially with the provincials. These were commonly eight by ten to ten by twelve feet, with two-foot high walls. Again, they were commonly scalloped-edged. Wall tents were usually set up like a marquee with only three poles, roping out the side walls of canvas. As the war progressed, officers were ordered to carry only a soldier's tent into the field. These, when the order was followed, were the six by nine foot bell-back tents. Tarps and flies were also erected for use by officers to keep them from the elements and increase living space. In general, the higher the rank, the more canvas and tentage officers had.

The other type of tent issued was the bell of arms. These tents were to house the arms. This was a cone-shaped tent with a single pole stretched outward by sixteen pegs to form a six by six foot shelter. The pole had cross pieces attached to support the men's muskets when racked inside. These were topped with a sheath of painted canvas or leather the color of the uniform's facings. Also, most regular regiments had their regimental cipher painted on the wall.

MESS KETTLES AND CAMP AXES. The other two items usually issued to each mess were a mess kettle and camp axe. The mess kettle was typically a ten-quart, straight-sided bucket used to collect and cook provisions. The vast majority of mess kettles were made of tin with canvas covers. The camp axe was a large, felling-type axe, used for cutting wood and general camp chores.

TOOLS FOR FIREARMS. Items expected to be carried by redcoats and some provincial units to take care of their muskets were hammer caps (hammer stall = leather sheath to fit over the frizzen of the lock to inhibit spark), stopper (a wood plug placed in the muzzle end of the musket barrel to keep out moisture), brush (animal hair brush to clean the pan of lock), wire (bent heavy wire to clean the touch hole of the musket lock), turnkey (screwdriver-type tool), oil bottle, rag, and a cover (cow's knee = leather to cover the lock of the musket to keep out moisture). To take care of the soldier's other gear, clothing, and equipment, regulars and some provincials were issued a clothes brush, a pair of shoe brushes, and black ball (a pasty-type substance to blacken leather), rags, and brick dust (to clean metal).

POLE ARMS were also common for officers and non-commissioned officers. In the early part of the war, officers carried a pike, called a spontoon or espontoon. These spear-like weapons were a symbol carried by both regulars and provincials. The non-commissioned officer carried a halberd. This pole arm was usually an axe-like weapon with a spear-shaped top. The halberd was not primarily symbolic but was an excellent tool for directing the men in training and parade maneuvers. Both arms were affixed to long wooden poles. As the Seven Years' War progressed, both of these pole arms were used primarily for parade and ceremony only. There were many orders for halberds not to be carried into the field but rather left in garrison.

OTHER ITEMS. For soldiers, this is about all they had. Other items they might have possessed were extra clothing, a cup, silverware, or personal belongings. Officers, on the other hand, traveled often with all the comforts of home. It was common for officers to have six to twelve changes of clothing, towels, chamber pots, tables, chairs, trunks, portmanteaus (leather cylindrical-shaped suitcases), china, crystal, liquor cabinets, books, cots or beds, mattresses, bedding, pillows, bolsters, various kitchen equipment, lanterns and servants to take care of everything. The higher the rank of an officer, the better he could equip himself.

MARKINGS. In order to keep all the clothing, gear, and equipment in the hands of the correct owner, markings were standardized as well. For the marking, worsted tape, black and red paint, brushes, and brands were employed. For clothing, the garment was directly painted on, or a piece of woolen tape was painted on and stitched inside the garment. Each man was issued a number, called a rack number, and all items had that number on it. All articles also had the regimental number, company (A = colonel's co., B = lieutenant colonels's co., C = major's co.), and a broad arrow

↑ GR, referencing it as King's issue (see Appendix 7).

The shirt, white, checked, or work smock, was painted directly on the outside lower right corner, while wearing the garment. The marking was about one and a half to two inches square.

Breeches, waistcoats, regimentals, and hats were not marked directly on the garment but rather on a piece of worsted tape stitched to the article. Breeches had the tape attached to the inside back at the side of the gusset. Waistcoats and regimentals had tape attached to the back inside neckline. Watch coats were to be marked under the cape on a piece of tape in red (no rack number because issued to the regiment). Hats were marked on a tape affixed to the inside back of the hatband.

Haversacks, knapsacks, snapsacks, packs, canteens (if wood or covered), and cartridge boxes were painted directly on the article in approximately a two-inch area. Articles with outer flaps were marked on the inside flap on the upper right flap corner, facing the open article. Canteens were marked on the side facing out in the center.

Belts, frogs, and slings were marked directly on the leather by painting the markings on the underside near the buckle. Markings on the items would vary because of the width of the leather.

Blankets were marked on the upper and lower left corners. Painted markings were placed directly on the blanket. Blanket markings were about eight inches square.

Tent markings were large and would be about ten inches square. The painted markings were directly on the linen. The lettering was placed on the outside wall, bottom left corner, facing the front of the tent on the right wall. The big difference is that tents were marked with the mess number, not the rack number, because tents were issued to 5-6 men and not individuals. Camp kettle bags were marked this way as well. Tent poles were branded with a broad arrow to represent King's issue.

Bayonets and swords were to be marked by engraving the company and rack number. The sword was marked near the hilt end of the blade. The bayonet was marked on the socket near the lip, parallel with the lip.

Muskets were more elaborately marked. Often there were ordnance marks on the barrel, markings for the lock's origin, date of making, and the British broad arrow was on the lock. The company and rack numbers were engraved on the escutcheon and butt plates.

Other items were marked as well. Both the King's and colonial stores had to be closely administered with strict

accountability.   Soldiers were answerable to any missing
equipment.   Ranger units, bateaux men, wagoners, and
Independent companies were also issued items.   These items
would have been marked, but speculation on these markings
are not substantiated in existing research materials.[6]

[6] Linda Baumgarten, *Eighteenth-Century Clothing at Williamsburg*
(Williamsburg, Va.: The Colonial Williamsburg Foundation, 1988);
John M. Bingeman, "Interim Report on Artifacts Recovered From
Invincible (1758) Between 1979-1984." *The International Journal of
National Archaeology and Underwater Exploration,* 14: 3 (1985) 191-
210; C. Willett and Phillis Cunnington, *Handbook of English Costume
in the Eighteenth Century* (Boston: Plays, Inc., 1972); Anthony
Darling, *Red Coat and Brown Bess* (Alexandria Bay, N.Y.: Museum
Restoration Service, 1991); Philip Weaver, "Belles De Armes," *French
and Indian War Magazine,* 1994, Photocopy, courtesy of Andrew
Gallup, in Author's Private Collection, Houghton Lake, Mich.; Jacob
L. Grimm, "Archaeological Investigation of Fort Ligonier, 1960-
1965" *Annals of the Carnegie Museum, Pittsburgh, Penn.,* vol. 42,
1970; Brenton C. Kemmer, *Freemen, Freeholders, and Citizen
Soldiers, an Organizational History of Col. Jonathan Bagley's
Regiment, 1755-1760* (Bowie, Md.: Heritage Books, Inc., 1997);
Brenton C. Kemmer, *Regimental Sketchbook of Clothing, Gear, and
Equipment, Col. Jonathan Bagley's 3rd Massachusetts Regiment,
Company C* (Houghton Lake, Mich.: The Living Historian, 1995);
Elisabeth McClellan, *Historic Dress in America, 1607-1870,* vol. 1
(Salem, N.H.: Ayer Co., Publishers, 1969); George C. Neumann and
Frank J. Kravic, *Collector's Illustrated Encyclopedia of the American
Revolution* (Texarkana, Tex.: Rebel Publishing Co., Inc., 1975); "An
Essay on Castramentation, by Lewis Lochee, London, 1778,"
Photocopy, courtesy of Jerry Olson, Author's Private Collection,
Houghton Lake, Mich.; Barton Redmon, unpublished paper on the
Uniform of the British Army, 1997, copy, courtesy of Barton Redmon,
in Author's Private Collection, Houghton Lake, Mich.; Sean
Shesgreen ed., *Engravings by Hogarth* (N.Y.: Dover Publications,
Inc., 1973); Scott Stephenson, "Gaiters, Leggings, or Spatterdashes,"
Standing Orders British Regular Regiments 1754-1764 Newsletter,
vol. 1 #5, May 1, 1989, p. 3-5; Norah Waugh, *The Cut of Men's
Clothes, 1600-1900* (London: Faber and Faber Limited, 1964);
Williams College Archives, Williamstown, Mass., 1995, Fisher Howe
Collection Box 1, F1, p. 4-6, "Battle of Lake George, Blodget's

Head coverings —
shoes were hard to
Replace.
Much wear and tear
to uniforms.
The material was sold
To the army - to the soldier
and made up by a Tailor.
Most enlisted men
wore civilian
clothes — Officers
provided & paid for
their uniforms.

Perspective Plan re-drawn and re-engraved by Thomas Jeffreys,
London, Feb. 2, 1756." (Hereafter cited as Blodget - Jeffreys, 1756.)
Photocopy, Author's Private Collection, Houghton Lake, Mich.;
Williams College Archives, Williamstown, Mass., 1995, Fisher Howe
Collection Box 1, F1, p.2-3, "Battle of Lake George, Perspective Plan
of the Battle of Lake George by Samuel Blodget, Engraved by Thomas
Johnston, Boston, Sept. 8, 1755." (Hereafter cited as Blodget -
Johnston, 1755.) Photocopy, Author's Private Collection, Houghton
Lake, Mich.; Williams College Archives, Williamstown, Mass., 1995,
"Inventory Written by Thomas Williams of Clothes and Sundries
found in Ephraim Williams' Chest at Lake George," Dwight
Collection, p. 44, Photocopy, Author's Private Collection, Houghton
Lake, Mich.

Part III

YANKEE PROVINCIALS

The largest group of British troops in the Lake George–Lake Champlain Corridor were men from Massachusetts, Connecticut, New York, New Jersey, New Hampshire, and Rhode Island. These Yankees put thousands into the field annually. Some colonies enlisted as many as two-thirds of all eligible men in their colony during the war. There were no warrants for the uniforming and equipping of these men, and each colony issued what they wanted when they wanted to. Consequently, each colony's troops had a distinctive appearance on the field. There was no uniformity achieved for the colonial troops during the war. Some colonials looked very regimental, and some looked like everyday men off the streets or from the colonial trainbands.

MASSACHUSETTS GEAR AND EQUIPMENT. Massachusetts Bay was probably the most militaristic of all of King George's colonies. Every year of the war, the Bay Colony sent more men to battle the French in America than any colony or regiment of the British army. These men were everywhere and made up one of the best-trained and equipped units in the provincial army.

MASSACHUSETTS REGIMENTS IN 1755. Massachusetts undoubtedly was one of the wealthiest colonies, as is shown by the issuance of gear and equipment (see Fig. 4). In 1755, the Bay Colony men marched to Lake George carrying blankets, knapsacks, haversacks, hatchets or swords, some cutlasses, tumplines, powder horns, bullet bags, worms and wires, Brown Bess muskets, bayonets, and slings. Massachusetts camps,

Fig. 4. On the left is a field officer of Massachusetts. The man on the right is a company grade officer with his spontoon. In the center is a private soldier.

although set up haphazardly, had a regimental look because of the issuance of wedge tents for men, wall tents for officers, and their regimental flags.[7]

MASSACHUSETTS REGIMENTS: 1756. In 1756, the Yankees of Massachusetts were issued powder horns, cartridge boxes, blankets, knapsacks, wooden bottles or canteens, bowls, spoons, King's arms (Brown Bess), bayonets, and slings. Each mess of six Bay boys was issued a tent, platter, kettles (some brass but mostly tin), and an axe. Other items of bedding were issued for their barracks like a bed sack, sheets, pillows, and lanterns. Great coats were supplied for the guards.[8]

MASSACHUSETTS REGIMENTS: 1757. As is shown in the excellent support of the Massachusetts House of Representatives, this colony's regiments continued their uniformity of equipment supply into middle war. In 1757, men were supplied with knapsacks, hatchets, tin flasks or canteens,

---

[7] "The Journal of Capt. Nathaniel Dwight of Belchertown, Massachusetts, During the Crown Point Expedition, 1755," (New York Genealogical and Biographical Record, 33 (1902) 5; *Acts and Resolves, Public and Private, of the Province of the Massachusetts-Bay* (Boston, 1908) 15: 264, 266, 304, 352, 386, 387. (Hereafter cited as *A&R*); *Journal of the House of Representatives of Massachusetts* (Boston: Massachusetts Historical Society, 1956) 34, part 1: 170 (Hereafter cited as *JHR*); *The Journal and Papers of Seth Pomeroy, Sometime General in the Colonial Service,* Louis Effingham de Forest, ed. (New Haven, Connecticut, 1926) 112; Perry, 343; Williams College Archives, Blodget - Jeffreys, 1756; *Pomeroy,* 121-22.

[8] Parkman, 224-225; Albert B. Hart, ed., *Commonwealth History of Massachusetts* (New York: Russell & Russell, 1966) 2: 433; Kemmer, *Freemen,* 36; *Samuel Greenleaf Journal 1756-1767,* Pre-Revolutionary Diaries 1635-1774 (Boston: Massachusetts Historical Society) microfilm reel 4, October 18, 1756; Cecil C. P. Lawson, *A History of the Uniforms of the British Army,* 3 vols. (London: Peter Davies, 1941) 3: 195; *Military Collector and Historian* 18 #2 (Summer 1991) Plate 669.

powder horns, bullet pouches, muskets, bayonets, kettles, and tents.[9]

MASSACHUSETTS REGIMENTS: 1758-1760. In the second half of the war, men from Massachusetts serving in the Lake George–Lake Champlain Corridor were well-equipped. The government along with King's stores, allotted these soldiers knapsacks or snapsacks, tin flasks or wooden bottles (one hop), tumplines, blankets, hatchets or swords, powder horns, cartridge boxes, and usually a musket. In 1758, a bounty was offered if soldiers brought their own arms or blankets. Each mess received their tent, a small wood axe, kettles (1-2), and flesh brushes for brushing off the salt from dried meat. Many of the tents were being supplied from British regiments. In 1759 and 1760, the 27th Regiment of Foot and the Royal Artillery supplied, for example, marquees for Massachusetts. This later part of the war also documents drums, flags, and sergeant's halberds.[10]

---

[9] Kemmer, *Freemen*, 36; American Antiquarian Society, "Order for 404 Coats," French and Indian War, Manuscript Box, Folder 8, 1756-1757-undated.

[10] Kemmer, *Freemen*, 37, 38, 39, 48, 49; *JHR*, 34, part 2: 417, 419; *Ibid.*, 35, part 2: 274, 287, 335; John Cleaveland to Mary Cleaveland, August 11, 1758, *John Cleaveland Papers* (Salem: Essex Institute, 1974, microfilm) 1; "Amos Richardson's Journal, 1758," *The Bulletin of the Fort Ticonderoga Museum*, 12 #4 (May 1979): 271, 281; "Petition of Ruth Farmer, 1758," *Ibid.*, 2 #2 (July 1930): 79; Paul O. Blanchette, ed., *Captain William Sweat's Personal Diary of the Expedition Against Ticonderoga* (Salem: Essex Institute, Historical Collections, 1957) 93: 38-39; Nick Westbrook notes, Abercromby Papers, Huntington Library, San Marino, Ca., Nov. 1995, #AB350, Pownall to Abercromby, 6/12/1758, Pell Research Center, Fort Ticonderoga, Ticonderoga, N.Y.; "Captain Thomas Lawrence's Company, an Inventory List of Clothing and Gear From Deceased Soldiers," *Massachusetts Historical Society, Proceedings* (Boston: Massachusetts Historical Society, May 1890) 25: 26-29; John A. Schutz, *Thomas Pownall, British Defender of American Liberty* (Glendale, Ca.: The Arthur H. Clark Co., 1951) 127; Joseph Nichols

MASSACHUSETTS UNIFORMS. The Bay Colony's soldiers' uniforms changed very little from the beginning to the end of the war. Men were issued shirts, shoes, red breeches and waistcoats, soldier's hats, and blue regimentals with large round cuffs and a blue scalloped arm flap. The red lapels were straight cut and had six buttons on each lapel.[11]

In 1756, soldiers received the same clothing with the addition of stocks, stockings, caps, and great coats. The great coats were issued to Col. Jonathan Bagley's men, garrisoned at Fort William Henry. Also that year, men were issued blue breeches instead of red.[12]

The year of the fall of Fort William Henry, Massachusetts men were given three shirts, two pair of shoes, and two pair of stockings. The rest of the uniform had not changed. On a receipt for regimentals in 1757, the men's coats were ordered

Diary (Henry E. Huntington Library, San Marino, Ca.) MS. HM89, 12, microfilm; *Orderly Book and Journal of Major John Hawks,* Hugh Hastings, ed. (Syracuse, N.Y.: Society of Colonial Wars, 1901) 7, 64; *A&R,* 16: 313, 722-23; "Journal of Sergeant Holden," *Massachusetts Historical Society, Proceedings* (Boston: Massachusetts Historical Society, 1899) 388; American Antiquarian Society, "Acct. of the 2nd Billeting Money Which Have Been Paid out and to Whome, As Also Blankets, Knapsacks, etc." French and Indian War Collection, M55 Boxes F, Folder 8; "Samuel Jenks, His Journal of the Campaign in 1760," *Massachusetts Historical Society, Proceedings* (Boston: Massachusetts Historical Society, 1890) 5: 375.

[11] Kemmer, *Freemen,* 42; Parkman, 171; John A. Schutz, *William Shirley, King's Governor of Massachusetts* (Chapel Hill: The University of North Carolina Press, 1961) 211; *A&R,* 15: 386; *JHR,* 34, part 1: 170; *Pomeroy,* 112, 143-44.

[12] Kemmer, *Freemen,* 35; Albert W. Haarmann, "American Uniforms During the French and Indian War, 1754-1763," *Military Collector and Historian,* vol. 32 #2, Summer 1980, 58; Hart, 433; *The Boston Weekly News-Letter,* 13 May, 1756.

unlined and red-faced in small, medium, and large. The officers' coats were to be lapelled in scarlet.[13]

The last two years, 1759 and 1760, saw the Massachusetts men in the same issuance. In 1759, the drummers' coats were to be green, and corporals were to wear yellow knots on their left shoulders. The big change in 1760 was in facings. The colony saw a need to distinguish the separate regiments of the colony, so each was issued a different facing color. The first regiment's uniforms were faced blue, the second red, and the third green.[14]

MASSACHUSETTS OFFICERS' UNIFORMS. The officers of Massachusetts tended to have a separation of uniform between company grade officers and field officers. Ensigns, lieutenants, and captains wore blue, scarlet-faced regimentals with gold buttons. To further distinguish their rank, they wore gold lace on their waistcoats and tricorns. Majors, lieutenant colonels, colonels, and generals were primarily seen in red, non-lapelled coats with large, round red cuffs. They wore gold lace on their waistcoats and hats, and some individuals also laced their regimentals (see Appendix 8).[15]

---

[13] Kemmer, *Freemen*, 36; Haarmann, p. 59; *Boston Weekly News-Letter*, 3 March and 22 Dec., 1757.

[14] Kemmer, *Freemen*, 47, 48; Captain John Knox, *The Historical Journal of the Campaigns in North America for the Years 1757, 1758, 1759, and 1760.* 3 vols. (Toronto: The Champlain Society, 1914) 1: 306; *Hawks*, 11; *A&R*, 16: 721-23; Acct. of the 2nd Billeting; "Extracts From Gibson Clough's Journal" (Salem: Essex Institute, Historical Collections, 1861) 3: 102; "Diary Kept at Louisbourg, 1759-60, by Jonathan Procter of Danvers," (Salem: Essex Institute Historical Collections) 70 (1934) 57.

[15] Kemmer, *Freemen*, 36, 47, 48, 63, 75, 79, 84, 85.; Lawson, 3: 195; *Military Collector and Historian* 18 #2 (Summer 1991) Plate 669; Henry W. Foote, *Portraits in the Essex Institute, Salem* (Salem, Mass.: Essex Institute, 1936) 127-28; Unknown artist, oil painting of Lt. Col. David Mason, 1726-1794, accession number 130, 763, gift of S. Prescott Fay, Peabody Essex Museum, Salem, Mass.

CONNECTICUT GEAR AND EQUIPMENT. The second largest amount of colonial manpower raised from the American trainbands came from Connecticut. This New England colonial force played a monumental part in combat and labor alike. For combat, the Connecticut soldiers received ample battle gear (see Fig. 5).

CONNECTICUT REGIMENTS IN 1755. In 1755, soldiers were issued blankets, knapsacks, cartridge boxes, powder horns, axes or swords, and tents. It appears that most men furnished their own musket.[16] The tents as chronicled in Samuel Blodget's drawing of the Battle of Lake George, were "ill made, not waterproof."[17]

CONNECTICUT REGIMENTS: 1756. In 1756, men were issued King's arms and accouterments. Capt. Thomas Williams' company of Colonel Fitch's Regiment were ordered to mark their firelock number XVII and brand their breech N.Y.[18] Part of the accouterments issued were cartridge boxes and either an axe or sword.[19]

CONNECTICUT REGIMENTS: 1757. In 1757, the colonies' provincials were again issued the Brown Bess musket. That year, it was recorded that these muskets were being cut down.

---

[16] Parkman, 171; Phone interview from Brenton C. Kemmer to John Eric Nelson, Milford, Conn., 9/2/97; *The Public Records of the Colony of Connecticut From May 1757 to March 1762 inclusive* (Hartford, 1850-1890) 10: 344. (Hereafter cited as *Conn. Records*); Williams College Archives, Blodget - Jeffreys, 1756.

[17] Stanley Pargellis, *Military Affairs in North America, 1748-1765* (New York: D. Appleton-Century Co., 1936) 141.

[18] Gary Zaboly, *Descriptions of Military Uniforms and Equipage in North America, 1755-1764, From Deserter Reports and Other Sources,* p. 3, Photocopy, courtesy of David Schmid, in Author's Private Collection, Houghton Lake, Mich.; *Conn. Records,* 22; *New-York Gazette, or Weekly Post-Bay.* 30 Aug., 1756.

[19] Fred Anderson, *A People's Army, Massachusetts Soldiers and Society in the Seven Years' War* (New York: W.W. Norton and Co., 1984) 174; John Eric Nelson interview, 9/2/97.

Fig. 5. The soldier on the right is an officer of the Connecticut Regiment. The man on the left is a private soldier in full marching kit. Notice the hair-on knapsack. The man in the center is wearing the fatigue dress for this colony, checked trousers and shirt.

The "Bess" normally was fitted with a forty-six inch barrel. Archaeologists found quite a number of four to eight inch barrel ends on Rogers' Island at Fort Edward. Part of these barrel ends can be attributed to Connecticut soldiers. Phineas Lyman, in his orderly book, records an order, "that ye men who are warned for guard appear clean dressed and well-shaved with ramrods a proper length for their guns."[20] Evidently, the soldiers or armorers of the colony were not reducing the length of the musket's ramrods to coordinate with the barrel length. This would be essential to allow the muzzle open encumbrance for loading.

CONNECTICUT: MESS GEAR. Each mess (six men) in 1755 was issued a wedge tent. Officers were issued marquees or wall tents. The tent mates (mess mates) adopted the cold-weather practice of building chimneys for the tents. This was done by dry-laying brick or stone chimneys at the rear of the linen tents. The best depiction comes from Phineas Lyman's orderly book of October 9, "that officers of ye several companies in ye Connecticut regiment are to take special care that ye men of their several companies build their chimneys in such a manner as will best secure ye men's health, prevent damage in their tents and clothes and make ye most decent and soldier-like appearance that is possible."[21] This chimney-building practice was widespread in the Yankee corps.

CONNECTICUT GEAR: 1758. The best documentation for gear in the Connecticut regiments comes from the first Ticonderoga expedition of 1758. That year, these New Englanders were issued the King's arms if they did not bring their own musket.

---

[20] *The Diary of Jabez Fitch Jr. in the French and Indian War, 1757.* (Fort Edward, N.Y.: Earl and Jean Stott. Third ed., 1986) 34; Chris Fox to Brenton C. Kemmer, 1991; *Phineas Lyman Orderly Book, 1757*, p. 49, Photocopy, courtesy of Chris Fox, in Author's Private Collection, Houghton Lake, Mich.; Earl and Jean Stott, *Exploring Rogers' Island* (Fort Edward, N.Y.: Earl and Jean Stott, 1986) 25.

[21] *Fitch*, 25, 28; *Lyman*, 9, 26, 106.

They were also issued cartridge boxes or shot bags and powder horns, axes or swords, knapsacks, blankets, and tents. Although that campaign was well-equipped, the British army had great difficulties supplying these equipages until, finally in June, the shipment of items arrived in Albany from England. Abercrombie wrote to the colonial governors issuing orders to impress equipment. The Connecticut government offered bounties for men with their own items subject, "to the expectance of the muster master."[22]

CONNECTICUT GEAR: 1759-60. The last two years of fighting in the corridor saw similar equipage of the Connecticut troops. Men received or brought for a bounty muskets, bayonets, cartridge boxes or shot bags and powder horns, axes or swords, knapsacks, blankets, and tents.[23]

CONNECTICUT UNIFORMS. Most years of the war found Connecticut soldiers in regimental uniform. At the beginning of the war, the colony did not issue regimentals. It had been a long-standing ritual for many of the militias to have militia coats and uniforms. Because of this constant, many of the colony's troops took the field in their militia uniforms in 1755 and 1756.[24]

In 1756 Connecticut provincial uniforms started appearing consistently. There are records of soldiers purchasing regimentals, and Capt. Thomas Williams' company of Colonel Fitch's regiment was just one of many units in regimentals. Also in 1756, Colonel Whiting wrote to William Johnson, concerned about winter clothing. "It is time me thinks, they

[22] *Conn. Records,* 94, 122, 123, 124; John Eric Nelson interview, 9/2/97; John Shy, "James Abercromby and the Campaign of 1758," unpublished, University of Vermont master's thesis, June 1957, Photocopy in Author's Private Collection, Houghton Lake, Mich.; 59, 84, 86.

[23] *Conn. Records,* 223, 244, 350; John Eric Nelson interview, 9/2/97; Zaboly, *Descriptions,* 4.

[24] John Eric Nelson interview, 9/2/97; Pargellis, 141.

(the garrison of Fort Edward) should have winter clothing, if they are to have any. I have repeatedly wrote to the commissioners and Mr. DePeyster. Why they are not sent, I know not. I believe some of them would have gone off before now were they not really satisfied that I had done everything in my power to get their clothing."[25]

The transition years of 1757 and 1758 show Connecticut troops receiving hats, shoes, stockings, regimentals, shirts, and small clothes. There were variations in the uniform for those years, and until the end of the war, Connecticut troops were seen in red coats faced with yellow, or blue coats faced with red.[26]

It was also during that time when Phineas Lyman chronicled an attempt to improve the appearance of these part-time soldiers. This may have been an attempt to squelch the complaints of regular officers, or it could have been attributed to his experience of soldiering for several consecutive years, telling him to make improvements. "The men ordered for duty are always to appear with their hats cocked and with shoes and stockings on before they march to ye grand parade."[27]

CONNECTICUT OFFICERS' UNIFORMS. A painting of Col. Nathan Whiting, commander of the second Connecticut regiment, gives us an excellent example of an officer's uniform. Whiting is clothed in a white ruffled shirt, scarlet breeches, white gaiters with black garters, black shoes, black hair bag with attached cravat, yellow waistcoat laced in scalloped silver, scarlet regimental with silver buttons and slashed cuffs faced with yellow, powdered wig, crimson net silk officer's sash,

[25] Zaboly, *Descriptions*, 3; William H. Hill, *Old Fort Edward Before 1800*. (Fort Edward, N.Y.: Privately printed by the Author, 1929) 102.

[26] *Lyman*, 63; Ian K. Steele, *Betrayals, Fort William Henry and the "Massacre"* (New York: Oxford University Press, 1990) 34.

[27] *Fitch*, 44; *Lyman*, 2, 49, 63.

black felt tricorn laced in silver, silver gorget on a yellow ribbon, and a silver mounted epee-style sword.[28]

Records from 1759 state that a soldier was to "receive one month's advanced pay with a good blanket and knapsack, and also a bounty of 35 shillings to be improved by each man to purchase a lapelled coat."[29] Several deserter reports cite red, yellow faced uniforms with red small clothes, checked trousers and shirts.[30] Most historians believe that the Connecticut regimental coat had a slash cuff and square tab cut lapel.[31]

The checked trouser and shirt seem to have been unique to Connecticut. There are many references to checked shirts being issued to many different regiments but not checked trousers. These colony troops were receiving a set of work clothes (shirt and trousers) made of checked, linen flannel.[32]

The British commanders in America had been trying to instate one provincial uniform for all colonies. Their hopes were to see all the American troops uniformed in a blue, red faced coat (similar to Massachusetts' coats) opposite of the regulars. The year 1760 saw Connecticut consciously making this change. The issue uniform for that year was dark navy faced with red, with lapel and cuff shapes similar to earlier Connecticut uniforms. Soldiers were also issued red small clothes to give them a good uniformed appearance. Again, the men were given a bounty to purchase their lapelled coats (see Appendix 9).[33]

---

[28] Robin May, *Wolfe's Army,* Men at Arms Series (London: Osprey Publishing, 1974) p. 42 and plate (B2); Sir William Johnson, *The Papers of Sir William Johnson* (Albany: The University of the State of New York, 1962) 13: 50.

[29] *Conn. Records*, 223.

[30] Haarmann, 58; *The Connecticut Gazette* (New Haven) 7 July 1759; *The Boston Evening-Post* 24 May 1762.

[31] John Eric Nelson interview, 9/2/97.

[32] *Fitch*, 44; Haarmann, 58; John Eric Nelson interview, 9/2/97.

[33] *Conn. Records*, 350; Zaboly, *Descriptions*, 4.

NEW YORK REGIMENTS. The third largest group of provincials was furnished by New York. Yorkers were seen in blue regimentals throughout the entire war. In 1755 and 1756, men were issued blue, red-faced regimentals, blue waistcoats, blue breeches, felt hats, shirts, two pair of oznaburg [*sic*] trousers, stockings, and a pair of shoes (see Fig. 6). In 1756, there were fifty-five great coats sent to Fort Edward for the New York troops garrisoned there for their guards. For battle, soldiers had arms, hatchets, cartridge boxes, and blankets. For some years of the war, Yorkers received King's arms, but many brought their own for a bounty.[34]

Although regimentals were still referred to in the later war, it appears that the majority of New York regiments were wearing dark, drab-colored coats with medium drab facings (1759-60). Drab was a greenish-yellow color. Most Yorkers were also issued buckskin breeches and waistcoats. To finish off the New York uniform, each soldier was issued dark, worsted stockings, shoes, and a felt hat.[35]

In 1755, William Johnson, commanding the Yorker troops and the expedition against Fort St. Frédéric, was clothed in a red, red-faced regimental edged in gold braid. Johnson's small clothes were blue with a crisscross of gold braid on his waistcoat. This gave him a reverse of his soldiers, a look very common of provincial officers. His uniform was finished off with a gold laced tricorn.[36]

---

[34] Zaboly, *Descriptions*, 8, 9; Phone interview from Brenton C. Kemmer to Eric Lorenzen, Marmora, Ont., Canada, 9/97; Lawson, 3: 200; Hill, 102.

[35] Lawson, 3: 201; William Nelson, ed. *Documents Related to the Colonial History of the State of New Jersey, Extracts From American Newspapers, Relating to New Jersey, 1756-1761* (Paterson, N.J.: The Call Printing and Publishing Co., 1898) 20: 99. (Hereafter cited as *N.J. Documents*); Zaboly, *Descriptions*, 8.

[36] Parkman, plate 24; Brian Leigh Dunnigan, *Siege 1759: The Campaign Against Niagara* (Youngstown, N.Y.: Old Fort Niagara Assoc., Inc., 1986) 63.

Joe Lee
97

Fig. 6. The officer on the right is Sir William Johnson, commanding not just the New York Regiment, but, the entire 1755 Corridor campaign. The other two men are private soldiers of the colony. Notice the issued trousers on the soldier on the left.

Fig. 7. Notice the two different uniforms of the New York Independents. The man in the center is uniformed in the standard red faced with green uniform of the Independent Regiments. The soldier on the right is wearing the short green faced with green uniform. The gentleman on the left is an officer of the unit.

NEW YORK INDEPENDENTS. New York also had several hundred Independent company soldiers in the corridor during the war. There appear to have been two uniforms documented on the Yorker Independents (see Fig. 7). One uniform was a red regimental with green facings. This was a standard coat for most Independent companies according to the 1751 Uniform Warrant.[37]

Also, throughout the war, a short green jacket with buckskin breeches shows up a lot. These were issued to Captain Cruikshank's (Crookshank's) company. It is possible his company wore the short green coat while Captain Rutherford's company were issued the red, green-faced regimental. Captain Cruikshank's men also had a problem with their arms. It seems his men's muskets ranged from six foot-six to scarcely four foot-six (see Appendix 10).[38]

NEW JERSEY REGIMENTS. The other three colonies sent less than half as many men as did Massachusetts, Connecticut, or New York. New Jersey was the fourth largest supplier of provincial manpower. Although not high in number, New Jersey may have been the best equipped unit in the Yankee army (see Fig. 8). The New Jersey province saw to it that their soldiers were uniformed from head to foot. That tradition was begun in the 1740's when, because of their uniforms, they received their nickname, the Jersey Blues.

Each man was issued a blue, red-faced coat after the highland fashion. These were short coats with red round cuffs, blue scalloped arm flaps, and red, square-cut lapels. Each soldier was also given blue breeches made from the same fabric as his coat, a pair of ticken (some buckskin) breeches, red waistcoat, checked shirt (ticken breeches and checked shirts were for work), white shirt, two pair yarn stockings, two

---

[37] Gerry Embleton and Philip Haythornthwaite, "The British Infantry of the Seven Years' War," *Military Illustrated Past and Present.* #36, May 1991 (parts 1-3) 22-34; Haarman, 65.

[38] Zaboly, *Descriptions*, 8-9.

Fig. 8. New Jersey's soldiers were the best equipped of the colonial troops. Notice that New Jersey had the only colonial grenadier unit. On the right is the uniform of the Jersey Blues. On the left is an officer of New Jersey. The man in the background is dressed for fatigue.

pair shoes, tricorn with yellow binding, blanket, knapsack, hatchet, canteen, cartridge box, musket, white gaiters, tent and camp kettle per every five men, and two hundred camp axes for the regiment.[39]

In 1758, the colony of New Jersey also raised one hundred men to act as grenadiers. These men were uniformed and accoutered identically to the rest of regiment, except they were issued cloth mitre caps. These were blue with a plate and band of red with a painted front with the typical Hanoverian horse and crown cipher, topped with a white tassel.[40]

In regard to accouterments, the Neumann collection shows a cartridge box similar to one found at Sabbath Day Point where 350 Jersey Blues were slaughtered in 1757. The box is an 11 ¾ by 2 ¾ inch straight block with two rows of holes; one of twelve and one of eleven. There is a double black flap with a long overhang on the outer flap and a pocket under the block. There is a 2 ¼ inch linen strap attached.[41]

NEW JERSEY OFFICERS' UNIFORMS. Col. Peter Schuyler of New Jersey is shown in a painting in a blue regimental with scarlet round cuffs, scarlet straight lapels, and gold braid. He has on a long scarlet waistcoat and cocked felt hat, both laced in gold. Schuyler is wearing blue breeches, ruffled shirt, cravat, and carries a spindle gold-hilt sword.[42] "A few days ago (6/12/58), the New Jersey forces, of between 11-1200 of the likeliest well-set men of the purpose as has perhaps turned out on army campaign, passed by this place for Albany. They

[39] Lawson, 3: 199-200; *N.J. Documents,* vol. 20, p. 193, *Pennsylvania Gazette; Ibid.,* 6/12/58 *New York Mercury;* Zaboly, *Descriptions,* 8.

[40] Charles M.B. Gilman, *The Story of the Jersey Blues* (Red Bank, N.J.: Arlington Laboratory for Clinical and Historical Research, 1962); Lawson, 3: 199-200; John Mollo, *Uniforms of the Seven Years' War, 1756-1763* (N.Y.: Hippocrene Books, Inc., 1977) 30.

[41] George C. Neumann and Frank J. Kravic, *Collector's Illustrated Encyclopedia of the American Revolution* (Texarkana, Tex.: Rebel Publishing Co. Inc., 1989) 71.

[42] Lawson, 3: 200-01.

wear under Col. Johnson, all in high spirits; their uniform blue, faced with red, grey stockings, and buckskin breeches."[43] (See Appendix 11.)

RHODE ISLAND PROVINCIALS. In 1755, at the Battle of Lake George, Rhode Island had four companies under colonels Cole, Angelle, Babcock, and Francis. It appears there were no uniforms for these troops, only an order for clothing deemed necessary, and to charge the cost of the clothing to the soldiers (see Fig. 9). Apparently the soldiers carried their own arms, for which they received a fifteen-pound bounty.[44]

Rhode Islanders in 1756 were issued blankets, arms and accouterments, kettles, cloth and materials out of which tents could be made. If they were issued arms and accouterments, they received some sort of powder horn and bullet pouch or cartridge box to hold ammunition. Instead of issuing the men tents, the colony gave them cloth and materials to make the tents. If the men were lucky enough to get into barracks, they could sell the tent materials or return them to the colony.[45]

The Rhode Island Committee of War in 1757 spelled out the issue of clothing for the soldiers. Each man was given three good shirts, two pair of good stockings, two pair of good shoes, one good waistcoat, and other clothes that were sound and whole. They also specified these clothes were to be issued out of clothes already owned by the colony, and any others were to be charged to the soldiers. The committee also

---

[43] *N.J. Documents,* vol. 20, p. 219, *New York Mercury* 6/12/58.

[44] Howard M. Chapin, *Rhode Island in the Colonial Wars, A List of Rhode Island Soldiers and Sailors in the Old French and Indian War 1755-1762* (Providence: Rhode Island Historical Society, 1918) 4; John R. Bartlett, ed., *Records of the Colony of Rhode Island and Providence Plantations in New England* (Knowles, Anthony and Co., 1860) 5: 313, 419-20, 430-31.

[45] *Ibid.,* 5: 480, 538.

Fig. 9. The men of Rhode Island were not issued uniforms. These soldiers were issued clothing that was already in possession of the colony, or, the colony impressed or acquired as cheaply as possible whatever clothing was deemed necessary, then charged in back to the soldier.

Fig. 10. The New Hampshire colony had the worst-equipped troops in the corridor. As shown by these three men, each soldier basically wore his own clothing, and furnished the majority of his gear.

requested any family who could spare a blanket should send one with the soldiers.[46]

In the later part of the war, the soldiers continued to receive similar issues subject to the Committee of War. Men received blankets, knapsacks, arms, tents, shirts, caps, stockings, breeches, and flannel jackets. There are no specifications as to uniformity of these issues excepting that things not supplied by the crown were to be acquired in the cheapest way possible. It seems that although no uniformity was present, the Rhode Island troops were at least issued the bare essentials through the colony's purchasing or impressing clothing, gear, and equipment. It was also common practice for the British to furnish tents, arms, and accouterments from the King's stores to the colonists in the later part of the war.[47]

NEW HAMPSHIRE. New Hampshire had the worst-equipped colonial soldiers. These men did not even have the necessaries of a soldier (see Fig. 10). In 1755, the New Hampshire men either were issued blankets and arms or were given a bounty for their own. In 1756, the colony made one of its few efforts by purchasing three hundred stands of arms (musket, bayonet, and sling) for the five hundred men recruited for Lake George. Each volunteer also received a blanket, hatchet, and snapsack.[48]

In 1757, each New Hampshire man again was issued a blanket, hatchet, and snapsack. Governor Benning Wentworth addressed the Council of the Assembly of the House of New Hampshire Representatives in March stating, "the uniform

---

[46] *Ibid.*, 6: 24, 78.

[47] *Ibid.*, 6: 130, 145, 191-93; *Capt. Stewart's 42nd Regimental Orderly Book 1759-61*, p. 16, Photocopy, courtesy of Barton Redmon, Author's Private Collection, Houghton Lake, Mich.; Zaboly, *Descriptions*, 9.

[48] Phone interview, Brenton C. Kemmer to Jeremy Muraski, Green Bay, Wis., 9/97; *Journal of the House of New Hampshire,* copies of pages 32, 368, 376, 504-5, 508-9, 551, 568, 576-7, 600 in Author's Private Collection, Houghton Lake, Mich.

clothing in a regiment is almost as necessary as uniformity in discipline as it distinguishes the troops from common laborers and artificers, and be a means in some measure to prevent desertions, and if a method can be agreed upon, to effect a thing so expedient for the service, it will be agreeable to the Earl of Loudon that such a provision should be made."[49] The committee replied, "the government has already in hand a sufficiency of clothes for that service."[50]

For the rest of the war, there is never a mention of uniforms or of clothing being issued to the New Hampshire men. Speculation would be that as Rhode Island did, men were issued some necessary clothing without uniformity from the colony's war stores which had been purchased or impressed. In 1760, a number of men under Col. John Goffe's command were wearing nightcaps during the daytime so he had them issued felt hats to be uniformly cut and cocked to his discretion.[51]

---

[49] *Ibid.*, 376.
[50] Zaboly, *Descriptions*, 6.
[51] *Ibid.*; Jeremy Muraski interview, 9/97.

Part IV:

RANGERS
AND LIGHT INFANTRY

There were two types of rangers in the British army in the colonies: Colonial and Independent companies. Colonial ranger companies were used for scouting, escorts, skirmishes, and terrorism. The ranger units were in the corridor to seek out enemy parties and to escort wagons and bateaux around the lakes. All colonies had these companies. Some of the better known companies were Partridge's Rangers from Massachusetts, Putnam's Rangers from Connecticut, Dunn's Rangers from New Jersey, and Blanchard's ranging company from New Hampshire (see Fig. 11). These ranging companies were clothed and accoutered by their respective colonies.

PARTRIDGE'S MASSACHUSETTS RANGERS. Col. Oliver Partridge was commander of the Massachusetts Royal Hunters, also called Partridge's Light Infantry or Partridge's Rangers. Partridge did not uniform his men but rather clothed them in civilian attire.

BLANCHARD'S NEW HAMPSHIRE RANGERS. Col. James Blanchard of New Hampshire also led a non-uniformed unit of men from his colony. These soldiers were a company of men who were used to the woods. They ranged into the Lake George area in 1755, becoming one of the earliest and most beneficial reconnaissance units for the British army. One of the officers of that unit, Robert Rogers, was to become the most famous of all rangers.

PUTNAM'S CONNECTICUT RANGERS. Starting as early as 1755, Capt. Israel Putnam of Connecticut led his company of rangers to chase the enemy over the expanses of the corridor.

Fig. 11. The three soldiers shown are Colonial Rangers. The man in the center belongs to Dunn's Rangers of New Jersey; the man on the right belongs to Putnam's Rangers of Connecticut; the soldier on the left belongs to Partridge's Rangers of Massachusetts.

Putnam's Rangers stayed annually at the front beginning with the winter of 1755-56. Throughout the war, his troops were quartered on an island in the Hudson River across from Fort Edward. Some of Putnam's men were Mohican Indians. In August 1758, Putnam was taken prisoner and was tortured. He escaped and returned to his unit later in the war.

The only reference to a uniform comes in late war when Col. Eleazer Fitch's Regiment of Connecticut mentions a brown coat and green waistcoat for Putnam's men.[52] As with the other ranger units, these men were issued shirts, stockings, breeches, and wore either shoes or moccasins. Many men made leggins of wool or leather to protect their legs in the woods, and most of them used issued weapons and accouterments. Putnam's, like many Connecticut units, probably used cut-down Brown Bess muskets for their ranging service. The majority of ranging units wore tricorn hats or cut off the brims of their hats, making them into small round hats for the woods.

DUNN'S NEW JERSEY RANGERS. In 1757, New Jersey raised a second company of its frontier guards under Capt. Hezekiah Dunn. These men were forwarded to Lake George instead of remaining in New Jersey. This unit definitely received a uniform. As New Jersey was one of the best equipped and clothed provincial troops, this makes good sense. Each of Dunn's men received a green half-thick under-jacket, gray-lapelled kersey waistcoat to be worn over the jacket, buckskin breeches, two pair of shoes, two pair of stockings, and a leather cap. The leather cap was in the form of a jockey cap for woods warfare. Each man was also issued a hatchet, a good blanket, and a pack.[53] It also makes sense that Dunn's

---

[52] Zaboly, *Descriptions*, p. 4.

[53] May, p. 44 and plate (D2); Lawson, 3: 215; Phone conversation, Brenton C. Kemmer to Timothy J. Todish, Grand Rapids, Mich., 11/97; Ted Spring and George Bray III, *Sketchbook 56, The*

Rangers received, as did the other Jersey troops, shirts, canteens, cartridge boxes, and muskets (see Appendix 12).

INDEPENDENT COMPANIES OF RANGERS:

ROGERS' RANGERS. The other type of ranger unit was the Independent company. This type of ranger unit was under pay and supply of the King. In the Lake George Corridor, there was only one independent ranging company: Rogers' Rangers.

In 1755, Robert Rogers was in Blanchard's New Hampshire ranging company. When the army left for winter quarters, Putnam and Rogers volunteered to stay and act as reconnaissance units for Col. Jonathan Bagley's garrisons at Fort William Henry and Fort Edward. Rogers was ordered quartered at Fort William Henry that winter.

After a series of successful winter raids, Rogers was commissioned in March of 1756 to recruit an Independent company of rangers of sixty men (see Figures 12 and 13). Men were allowed ten Spanish dollars each, for clothing, arms and blankets. Most of the soldiers were probably clothed in frocks made of rough linen and carried shooting bags and powder horns.[54] Later that same year, Rogers was ordered to raise several new companies, one of Stockbridge Mohicans and two others in which each man received a good hunting shirt (workman's frock or smock), vest, breeches, Indian stockings (leggins), shoes, and hatchet. These two companies furnished their own blankets.[55] Out of the King's stores, they received muskets and cartridge boxes.

Highlanders and Provincial Rangers (St. Louis, Mo.: The Brandy Press, 1984) 3: 56, 62.

[54] Lawson, 3: 213; *Rogers' Journal*, 13.

[55] *Ibid.*, 19; Burt G. Loescher, *The History of Rogers' Rangers, The Beginnings, January 1755 - April 6, 1758* (San Francisco: Privately published by the Author, 1946) 1: 99, 115; Timothy J. Todish, Comments on the Uniform of Rogers' Rangers to Supplement a Lecture Given at the International Ranger Conference, Seven Eagles Outdoor Center, Grand Rapids, Oh., 1991, Photocopy in Author's Private Collection, Houghton Lake, Mich.

In 1757, there were two new companies raised, and Lord Loudon raised a company of cadets to learn woods warfare from Rogers and his officers. These cadets, after training, were to be placed in charge of light infantry companies, as regular officers in command of redcoat ranger units. Again, each man was given ten dollars for clothing and gear.[56]

In the Independent Companies of American Rangers, as Rogers' unit was labeled, in 1758, "each man was to provide himself with a good blanket and warm clothing the same to be uniform in each company."[57] The Indians were to be in their Indian dress. Rogers' contractor, Forsey, an Albany clothier, was to make regimentals, but they did not have enough green cloth so the clothiers Kennedy and Lyle, and Peble and Wiles were to make up the balance.[58] The green jackets were to be of serge and lapelled, cuffed and lined in frieze. The lapels were square cut, and the cuffs were round and small with a scalloped arm flap. The buttons were plain pewter. Rogers also ordered silver-laced tricorns and silver lace on the arm flaps of the officer's uniforms. The lace was to be small and square looped.[59] Several of Rogers' companies were issued different uniforms. It appears that Hobbs' and Speakman's may have been issued coats and waistcoats of grey duffel to be deducted from their pay.[60]

Rogers' unit was augmented to one thousand. He received a new company of Mohegan Indians from Connecticut. Rogers was commissioned a major on the sixth of April, 1758. The rangers also received packs or knapsacks, blankets, hats,

---

[56] *Rogers' Journal,* 35-36.

[57] *Ibid.*, 45.

[58] Loescher, vol. 1, 224.

[59] Mary C. Rogers, *A Battle Fought on Snow Shoes* (Derry, N.H.: Published privately by the Author, 1917) 11; Todish Lecture; Gary Zaboly to Timothy J. Todish, Remarks on Rogers' Rangers' Uniform Jacket, Nov. 1976, Photocopy in Author's Private Collection, Houghton Lake, Mich.; Spring and Bray, 1: 4, 14.

[60] Lawson, 3: 216-17; Rogers, 7.

Fig. 12. Rogers' Rangers had several different uniforms. The man on the left is clothed in a hunting or workman's shirt, a form of early uniform. The man on the right is wearing Rogers' famous 1758 green regimental. The man in the center is clothed in a gray duffel goat. Speakman's and Hobbs' companies of Rogers' Rangers may have received these.

Fig. 13. Here are two officers of Rogers' Rangers. The officer on the right is dressed in his field uniform. Notice the absence of silver lace except on the arm flaps. The officer on the left is wearing his dress or parade uniform, fully laced with his silver laced tricorn and gorget.

arms or bounty for them, hatchets, and some cutlasses. The hats varied from tricorns, round cut-down felt hats like sailors wore, felt jockey caps (favorites of officers), and the favorite of the soldiers, the highland bonnets. These bonnets were navy blue with a band of red wool. Many had a black cockade, button, and even fur.[61]

In 1759, Rogers' Rangers received special arms. In January, Rogers wrote to Mr. Cunningham, one of his contractors in New York, that the arms were in great need. Then, in February, Cunningham wrote back that they were on their way. There has been some speculation that these were light infantry muskets or small caliber cut-down carbines.[62] Rogers' unit was ordered on a terrorist retaliation expedition against the Abenaki Indian village of St. Francis in 1758. The equipment issued to his men gives us good picture of late war rangers. Each man was issued two pair of moccasins, two pair of footings, a pair of Indian stockings or leggings, hatchet, case (cartridge box) and belt, and tumpline.[63] Then, in October, Lieutenant Darcy of Rogers' unit was sent to pick up clothing and the necessaries sent for Rogers' corps from his clothiers and contractors in Albany.[64]

The thing to remember about Independent Ranger companies is that other than specifics such as Rogers' green coats, clothing and equipment were available or for sale to these units and all units under the King's pay. Consequently, Rogers' unit or individual men could further supply themselves as did redcoats. Additional clothing, equipment, gear, and

---

[61] Rogers, 2; *Rogers' Journal,* 49, 50, 53, 56; Lawson, 3: 216-17; Spring and Bray, 1: 42.

[62] John R. Cuneo, *Robert Rogers of the Rangers* (New York: Richardson & Steirman, 1987) 144; Spring and Bray, 1: 38; *Rogers' Journal,* 73-74.

[63] Loescher, vol. 2, 56.

[64] *Ibid.,* 66-67.

tentage were available to them with Rogers' signature, as with all other commanders (see Appendix 13).

LIGHT INFANTRY COMPANIES. As a result of the cadet company's training, the redcoat regiments formed light infantry companies officered by regular, trained officers. The most athletic and agile soldiers were selected from the regiments. Many modifications were made to prepare these new companies for service (see Fig. 14). At first, orders were given to modify existing uniforms. This was undertaken by cutting clothing short, removing regimental lace, and cutting down the tricorn hats. Further modifications were shown by example of the 60th Regiment's light infantry company's uniform. The men wore their issued shoes, hose, breeches, and shirts; everything else was modified. The sleeves were removed from the regimental coat and sewn onto the waistcoat, making a sleeved waistcoat. Then, the coat and waistcoat were shortened. The facings were left on the regimental and wings, similar to those on the shoulders of grenadiers were added, but these were fuller and longer, hanging half the way down the arm. Two small leather pockets almost breast high were added to hold extra ball and flint. Red wool flaps were added so the contents would not fall out. The sleeveless jacket was then to be worn over the fabricated, sleeved waistcoat. The tricorn was unlaced, and the brim was cut off except for a flap in the front that was buttoned up like a jockey cap. Enough black cloth was added to hook under the chin. Wool leggings were worn over the hose with leather straps passing under the arch of the shoes.[65]

Gear modification also occurred. The 60th Light soldier was to wear a belt axe with a rough, buttoned cover. This hung on a leather strap on the side between the coat and waistcoat. A cartridge box was worn on the left shoulder and a powder horn on the right. The knapsack was worn on a strap of

---

[65] Lawson, 2: 46-47.

Fig. 14. The Light Infantryman on the left is from the 42nd Regiment of Foot. The soldier on the right is from the 60th Regiment of Foot. Notice how they have adapted their waistcoats into sleeved garments and equipped themselves for woodland warfare.

Fig. 15. Here is an officer and an enlisted man of Lord Howe's 55th Light Infantry Regiment. Notice the shortened muskets and uniforms. The unit adapted to woodland uniforms while keeping the appearance of regular troops. Lord Howe was one of the army's biggest advocates of Light Infantry and Rangers.

webbing high on the middle of the back. Under that, on a narrow strap of webbing, was carried the canteen which was to be covered with cloth.

This was the general appearance for all light troops in regiments in the corridor. Commanding officers were given latitude to make the decisions to leave facings on the light infantry regimentals, but they were all to remove their regimental lace. Some companies removed their facings (cuffs and lapels), leaving a simple, sleeved waistcoat. Most men in light companies cut their tricorns either into jockey caps or into round hats, which were unlaced tricorns with the brims cut to only about two inches. Highland troops also made the coat modifications and wore breeches instead of kilts when not on parade or in camp.[66]

The muskets of the light infantry, like many muskets of regiments, were cut down for better maneuvering. Many of these companies were also issued special arms. The 1st, 27th, 42nd, 44th, and the 4th batt. 60th light infantry companies were issued French muskets in 1757-1758. These were smaller caliber and shorter weapons than the Brown Bess. Then, in 1759, these companies were ordered to turn in their French arms in exchange for British carbines. The new weapons were to have their barrels blued or browned to cut the glare of the metal.[67] These were probably similar to a light infantry carbine in a collection with a lock marked "Vernon," dated 1757. This musket is a sixty-five caliber instead of the standard seventy-five caliber. The barrel is forty-two inches long, rather than forty-six, and it weighs 7.1 pounds compared to the heavier, nearly 9-pound Brown Bess.[68]

---

[66] *Ibid.*, 46-47.
[67] "The Moneypenny Orderly Book," *The Fort Ticonderoga Museum Bulletin,* 12 (1966-1970) 328-357, 434-461 (2/26/59 and 5/6/59); Spring and Bray, 3: 31.
[68] Neumann and Kravic, 65.

LIGHT INFANTRY REGIMENTS. Another technique, rather than forming companies with the regular regiments for light infantry service, was the forming of light infantry regiments. **HOWE'S 55TH REGIMENT OF FOOT.** In 1755, the 57th Regiment was formed, and in 1757, it was renumbered the 55th Regiment of Foot. This was Lord Howe's Light Infantry Regiment (see Fig. 15). Howe, being one of the major advocates of light troops, patterned his unit as red-coated rangers. He drew from his own experiences on expeditions with American ranger units. Lord Howe's unit wore red coats with dark green facings. The lapels were squared, and the cuffs were a slash style. The regimental lace was yellow worsted tape. The 55th Light Infantry was ordered to cut their waistcoats and regimentals short. They also unlaced their tricorns and cut the brims to two and a half inches, forming a small round hat. Howe's regiment wore the other usual clothing of shoes, hose, gaiters, red breeches, shirts, and cravats. Howe and his officers laced their uniforms in gold.

Gear carried by this regiment included haversacks, knapsacks, blankets, canteens, shoulder-slung cartridge boxes, belly boxes for extra cartridges, hatchets, bayonets carried on a belt frog with the hatchet, and shortened muskets. Lord Howe even had his men crop their hair short.[69]

In 1758, Maj. Thomas Gage raised a regiment of light-armed men, the 80th Regiment of Foot (see Fig. 16). Gage recruited five companies in 1757 and 1758 for his regiment. This unit was to be uniformed more as rangers than light infantry redcoats. Their uniform consisted of shoes, hose, gaiters, brown breeches, brown short waistcoats, and brown short jackets with black buttons. This unit had no facings or lace. Their hats were cut-down tricorns, like jockey caps, and they may have had leather caps similar in style. For parade,

---

[69] Embleton, part 2, p. 36; May, p. 46-47 and plate (F2).

Fig. 16. Gage's Light Infantry was clothed in brown uniforms, looking similar to a ranger unit. The man on the left is an officer of the regiment. The soldier in the center is outfitted in full marching kit. The soldier on the right is wearing the late war uniform. This uniform had the addition of facings and a tricorn to more emulate other regular units.

officers may have had a gold lace coat and laced tricorn, as was common in ranger units.

The 80th was issued haversacks, knapsacks, canteens, belt frogs, belt axes, belly boxes, powder horns, bayonets, and shortened muskets. In 1759, the unit was issued carbines without bayonets. The rest of their uniform and gear stayed the same. In the early 1760's, near the end of the war, Gage's 80th Regiment was uniformed in standard, regular uniforms of red faced with orange.[70]

---

[70] Embleton, part 1, 22; *Ibid.*, part 2, 39; "British Light Infantry in the Eighteenth Century," p. 16, Photocopy, courtesy of Jerry Olson, in Author's Private Collection, Houghton Lake, Mich.; Parkman, plate 55; May, p. 46 and plate (F1); Lawson, 3: 207; *Moneypenny*, 5/5/59; Timothy J. Todish, *America's First First World War, The French and Indian War, 1754-1763* (Grand Rapids, Mich.: Suagothel Productions, Ltd., 1982) 50.

Fig. 17. The man in the center is a grenadier of the 1st Regiment of Foot. The man on the left is an officer of the regiment. The soldier on the right is in Parade Dress.

Part V:

THE REDCOATS

There were ten British regular (hat company) regiments in the Lake George–Lake Champlain Corridor during the Seven Years' War. Some, but not all of these, saw service on the front for the majority of the war. In 1759, the second battalion of the 1st Regiment of Foot, the Royals, were with Amherst's push north (see Fig. 17). They were commanded by Lt. Col. William Forster.

THE ROYALS were issued shoes, hose, blue wool breeches, shirts, cravats, red laced waistcoats, tricorns, both marching and dress gaiters, garters, and fatigue wear. As with all redcoat uniforms, the waistcoat for men five foot eight inches tall were to have nine buttons, men five foot nine inches wore eleven buttons, and grenadiers who were five foot eleven inches tall wore twelve buttons. The lace for the waistcoat was to be the same as on the coat, which for the 1st Regiment was plain white worsted tape. The regimental was red wool with blue, square lapels and slash cuffs. The coat was laced in a square loop with double lace on the cuffs. As with all regulars, there was to be no lace under the pocket flaps. The regimental of the Royals was to be hemmed two and five-eighths inches from the ground while the soldier was kneeling. The buttons were to be spaced a quarter-inch apart. Officers were to have narrow gold lace on their uniforms and gold banding on their hats. Grenadiers had no wings on the coats but wore a distinctive mitre cap. It was red with the usual blue band and ground with a circlet of St. Andrew with a yellow GR within.[71]

---

[71] A.E. Haswell Miller and N.P. Dawnay, *Military Drawings and Paintings in the Collection of Her Majesty The Queen* (London: Phaidon Press Ltd., 1966) 1: Morier #56. (Hereafter cited as *Morier*);

The gear issued to the Royals was standard to other regulars. Haversack, canteen, shoulder-slung cartridge box, belt frog, blanket, knapsack, sword, bayonet, and Brown Bess were issued. Each grenadier was equipped with a belly box for additional ammunition and wore a slow match (brass case with a match or wick inside for lighting grenades) attached to the leather strap of his shoulder-slung cartridge box.

THE 17TH REGIMENT OF FOOT also accompanied Amherst's 1759 army (see Fig. 18). These men were issued shoes, hose, marching and dress gaiters, garters, red breeches, shirts and necks (neck cloths), red waistcoats, tricorns, and regimentals. Regimental coats for this regiment were red with a grayish-white facing color. The lapel was square cut, and the cuffs were slash style. The coat was laced in pointed or bastion-shaped loops of white regimental tape with a double grey zigzag between two blue stripes. The waistcoat was looped and trimmed as well. Rather than the standard, scalloped coat pockets and arm flaps, the 17th had a unique fishbone style. The cuff had a double row of lace. Grenadiers had laced wings on the shoulders of the coat. The grenadier caps had the standard British cipher and Hanoverian horse design. Officers were to lace their uniforms and hats in silver braid.[72]

Gear was standard to the King's Warrant. Near the time of this regiment's appearance at Lake George (1758-1759), orders were being given for regulars to leave their swords in garrison and replace them with belt axes. The same was true for officers' and NCOs' pole arms. Officers were to take fuzees instead of the spontoon, and sergeants were to take muskets and bayonets instead of their halberds.[73]

Embleton, part 2, p. 32; Lawson, 2: 38, 40, 102; Liliane and Fred Funcken, *British Infantry Uniforms, from Marlborough to Wellington* (Tournai, Belgium: Casterman S.A., 1976) 16, 20.

[72] *Morier* #61; Embleton, part 2, p. 34; Lawson, 2: 103; Funcken, 16, 22.

[73] *Moneypenny,* 5/5/59; Lawson, 2: 46.

Fig. 18. These two soldiers are of the 17th Regiment of Foot. The grenadier on the right is a sergeant, distinguished by his waist sash. The private soldier on the left is dressed for inspection.

THE 27TH REGIMENT OF FOOT, OR THE INNISKILLINGS, reached the corridor in 1757 and stayed through the next three campaigns (see Fig. 19). They wore red regimentals with buff-colored facings. The lapels were square with slash cuffs. The grenadiers had square wings on the shoulders of their coats. The regimental lace was white wool with a yellow stripe in between a black and blue zigzag in square loops. The waistcoat was trimmed but not looped. The coat's pockets were scalloped, but the arm flaps were fishbone cut. The cuff had a single row of lacing. Officers laced their uniforms in silver in the 27th. The grenadier caps were embellished with the Hanoverian horse and a castle above, instead of the usual GR.[74]

The Inniskillings were also issued neck cloths, shirts, tricorns, red breeches, marching and dress gaiters, garters, hose, shoes, and fatigues. The standard gear was buff leather for knapsacks, cartridge box belts, and other belts. The cartridge box was black leather. As long as this regiment was on the frontier, it may have seen considerable modifications for woodland warfare such as the shortening of muskets, the wearing of leggins, and the use of axes instead of swords.

MONRO'S 35TH REGIMENT OF FOOT. Monro's regiment, the 35th Regiment of Foot, was one of the first redcoat units in the Hudson Valley. They arrived in 1756 and relieved the provincial army at Fort Edward and Fort William Henry (see Fig. 20). Monro's soldiers were supplied with shoes, hose, marching and dress gaiters, garters, red breeches, shirts, neck cloths, red waistcoats, tricorns, and fatigues. According to the 1751 Uniform Warrant, their regimental coat was red wool, faced with orange. The facings were square lapels and slash cuffs. The scalloped pockets had a double row of regimental lace. There was no arm flap but there was fishbone lacing on the arm. Regimental lace was white tape with a yellow

---

[74] Funcken, 18, 22; *Morier* #64.

Fig. 19. These three soldier are of the 27th Regiment of Foot. The officer (Ensign) on the right is holding the King's Colours of his regiment. The grenadier in the center wears his distinctive, ciphered, mitre cap. The soldier on the left shows the coat without wings, only distinctive on grenadier's coats.

Fig. 20. These three men are of the 35th Regiment of Foot. On the left is a grenadier, and on the right is a private soldier. The officer in the center is carrying his officer's spontoon.

Fig. 21. The 42nd Regiment of Foot, or Royal Highland Regiment is shown here by a private soldier on the left, a grenadier in the center, and an officer on the right. Notice the distinctive bear fur mitre cap of this regiment. The officer is shown in the late war issued coat with lapels.

zigzag inside a red and yellow stripe. The loops were square. The waistcoat was looped and trimmed. Officers of the 35th trimmed their uniforms with silver braid. Grenadier's coats had no wings on the shoulders, and their caps were the standard horse and GR pattern.[75]

Many of these men served in winter garrisoning of the corridor and so would have had to make modifications and additions to their uniforms and gear. They were issued King's equipment and gear according to army warrants and orders.

THE 42ND REGIMENT OF FOOT (ROYAL HIGHLANDERS). The 42nd Regiment of Foot, which came to be distinguished as the Royal Highland Regiment, arrived in 1756 and served in consecutive years of the war. This regiment was allowed to dress in their traditional, highland garb (see Fig. 21). Their regimental headdress was the highland bonnet. This was a navy, woolen, balmoral bonnet with a band of red wool and a red wool tassel on the top center. A black ribbon cockade with a pewter regimental button was worn on the left side of the bonnet. A piece of the blackest bear fur was worn on the left side of the bonnet reaching to the tassel. Many officers adorned their bonnets with black feathers. The 42nd grenadier caps were the only bear fur mitres allowed by the 1751 Uniform Warrant. They had a red wool plate in back and a red ground in front. This ground was embroidered in white with the Royal GR crown cipher without the Hanoverian horse.

The highland regiment was issued shoes and hose. The hose were a red and white woven cloth cut and sewn to the shape of the leg in what is called the harlequin pattern. They were held up by red woolen tape garters. The kilt was the issue brought over to America – the government sett that they were so proud to wear instead of breeches. The belted plaid (kilt or tartan, known to the highlanders as *breacan-an-fheilidh*) was made of many yards of plaid wool, which was

---

[75] Funcken, 18, 22; *Morier* #67.

laid upon the ground; the soldier would roll up in it, belt or pin it around his waist, and pin or tie the remaining yardage over his left shoulder. The pattern of the design of the government sett was blue, black, and green woven in plaids. There is some speculation that the grenadiers may have had an additional red thread running through their plaids. Soon after new plaids arrived, the old plaids were cut and tacked into a short kilt for around the waist, without the additional tartan over the shoulder (similar to a modern kilt). These were referred to as the *fheilidh beag* or little kilt.

The waistcoat and regimental were both red and cut short to accommodate the plaid. The facing color was buff from 1756-1758. Three days before the Battle of Ticonderoga, the regiment received its royal status, and the next issuance of uniforms were of blue facings (the regiment did not get the news of royal status until after returning from Ticonderoga). Highland regimental coat facings had no lapel until 1760. At that time, their new issuance were lapelled, having still the earlier style large round collar and round cuffs as well. The regimental lace was white with two red stripes. The looping on the coats were bastion-shaped but the waistcoats were only trimmed. The pocket on the coat was scalloped, and the arm flap was rectangular with four buttons. Officers laced their uniforms in gold, and sergeants may have laced theirs in silver in the early part of the war.

The gear issued to the 42nd was different as well. Armed with the Brown Bess, their weapons had black leather slings rather than tan/buff. They were also issued a black leather shoulder-slung baldrick, worn over the right shoulder, instead of the buff belt frog. This held the highland soldier's basket-hilt, broad sword. Each man was given a belly box for ammunition, but soon was given a shoulder-slung box as well. These soldiers carried their bayonets in a loop upon the belt of their belly boxes. Blankets were carried on tumplines. Several personal items were also carried by most of the 42nd.

A dirk or large knife was a typical highland weapon. Also, a sporran or leather bag was worn hanging in the front of the kilt from around the waist. This was to carry personal belongings, similar to a wallet or purse. Both the dirk and sporran were unissued and varied in design.

Because of the length of service, this regiment's modifications show good examples of changes in gear and equipment in North America. In 1759, over a thousand highland pistols were ordered for the regiment. The men had cut down their muskets, but they still had their swords. Officers were supplied with a new style tent, probably short-walled tents. In March, linen sailcloth breeches and blue wool leggins were ordered for the 42nd. An order in April had the men making hose from tartan rather than red and white fabric. Plaids were being used as sails in bateaux. The officers, as well, were modifying. They were to wear plain (unlaced) regimentals and boots when the men exercised.[76]

During this time of modification and change, there were constant orders to maintain regimental, highland dress. There were only certain times when a soldier could be in breeches and not his kilt, and in April of 1759, an order cites, "for review, the officers to be in kilt, plain regimentals, hair albermarld [sic], powdered and buff colored gloves, with their cartridge boxes on and everything else regimental. The men to be powdered. Their hair well-dressed, well-kilted [sic], new shoes, new hose, and everything else in perfect order."[77]

Both in April 1759 and January 1760, a list was given of what the men of the 42nd were to carry. In 1759, "Regimental order, the non-commissioned officers and soldiers are to carry with them to the field the following things viz. - 2 white shirts, 1 checked ditto., 1 spare pair of shoes, 2 pair of hose, 2 pair of socks, 1 pair of leggings, and 1 good pair of short canvas

[76] Funcken, 18, 22; *Morier #70*; *42nd Orderly Book,* 2/22/59, 3/18/59, 3/21/59, 4/7/59, 4/18/59, 5/17/59, 10/11/59.

[77] *Ibid.,* 4/18/59.

britches."[78] Then, in 1760, they were to take, "4 shirts, 2 pair of shoes, 3 pair of hose and leggins, 2 dimity stocks and buckles, 2 yards of black tape for their hair and red tape garters, with tumplines for their packs. Arms to be complete with stoppers, pickers, brushes, and hammer caps of black leather."[79]

JAMES ABERCROMBIE'S 44TH REGIMENT OF FOOT came over to Lake George in 1756-57, although members like William Eyre were in the corridor in 1755 (see Fig. 22). This redcoat unit was issued buff/tan belts, straps, and frogs, haversacks, canteens, blankets, cartridge boxes, swords (exchanged for axes), bayonets, and Brown Bess muskets.

For uniforms according to the warrant, the 44th received shoes, hose, both marching and dress gaiters, garters, red breeches, shirts, neck cloths, red waistcoats trimmed and looped, and red regimental coats faced yellow. The facings were square lapels and slash cuffs. The pockets on the coat were scalloped, and the arm flaps were rectangular. All was single laced. Regimental lace was white tape with a yellow stripe between a blue and black zigzag. Regimental lace loops were bastion-shaped with a distinctive diamond-shaped looping on the lapels. Grenadier coats had no wings, and their mitres were the standard horse and GR design. Officers laced their uniforms in silver.[80]

LASCELLE'S 47TH REGIMENT OF FOOT. The 47th Regiment of Foot, or Lascelles' Regiment, was in the Lake George–Lake Champlain Corridor in late war (see Fig. 23). They wore a red coat with white facings. Their facings were of square lapels and slash cuffs. The arm flaps were rectangular, and the pockets were scalloped. Grenadier coats had no wings, and their caps were the issued horse and GR style embroidery.

---

[78] *Ibid.*, 3/22/59.

[79] *Ibid.*, 1/18/60.

[80] Funcken, 18, 22; *Morier* # 71; Embleton, part 2, p. 36, 102-03; *Rogers' Journal,* 28; Steele, 70.

Joe Lee
97

Fig. 22. These soldiers of the 44th Regiment of Foot are on work detail. The sergeant on the left is standing guard and the man on the right is digging entrenchments. Notice the fatigue hat on the soldier on the right.

Fig. 23. The soldier of the 47th Regiment of Foot in the center is wearing his fatigue hat and work smock (shirt). The soldier on the left is a corporal distinguished by his white worsted shoulder knot. The gentleman on the right is an officer of the 47th Regiment of Foot.

The regimental lace for the 47th was white tape with a yellow stripe between two black zigzags looped in bastions. Officers' lace was silver. The waistcoat was laced and trimmed. All was single laced. This unit was issued red breeches and the standard clothing and gear according to orders and warrants.[81]

COL. DANIEL WEBB'S 48TH REGIMENT OF FOOT was issued red regimentals with buff facings (see Fig. 24). There were wings on the grenadier coats. The facings were square lapels and slash cuffs. The pockets and arm flaps were both scalloped, and all was single laced. The regimental lace was in square loops, and the waistcoat was looped in a unique diamond pattern and trimmed. The white worsted lace had a yellow stripe between a green stripe and green scroll pattern. Officers laced their uniforms in gold. The 48th used brass buttons on the uniform. The grenadier mitre cap was the issued, standard, warrant pattern. Equipment and gear were full and aligned to British army standards.[82]

THE 60TH REGIMENT OF FOOT: THE ROYAL AMERICANS. The 62nd Regiment of Foot was raised in 1755 of recruits from Massachusetts, New York, Pennsylvania, Maryland, and North Carolina. Many men were also from Swiss, German, and English ancestry. The regiment was known as the Royal American Regiment. In 1757 the Royal Americans were renumbered the 60th Regiment of Foot (see Fig. 25). The colonel of the regiment was Henry Bouquet.[83]

---

[81] Funcken, 18, 22; *Morier* #69; Embleton, pt. 2, p. 36; Lawson, 2: 102-03.

[82] Funcken, 18, 22; *Morier* #69; Embleton pt. 2, p. 36; May, p. 43 and plate (C1); Lawson, 2: 102-03.

[83] May, p. 48 and plate (H2); Lawson, 2: 209-10; Dr. Todd Harburn "A Most Unfortunate Officer," *Michigan History*, vol. 72 #2 (March/April, 1988): 45; Raymond A. Washlaski, "Regimentals and Leather Breeches, Military Dress of the French and Indian War Period," *French and Indian War Magazine,* 1990, Photocopy, courtesy of Terry Todish, in Author's Private Collection, Houghton Lake, Mich.

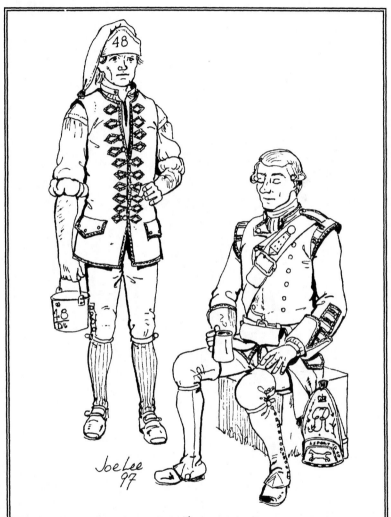

Fig. 24. The grenadier of the 48th Regiment of Foot is relaxing on the right. Notice how his regimental coat is buttoned across for marching. The soldier on the left is wearing his small clothes. Notice the distinctive diamond looping of his regimental lace.

Fig. 25. The 60th Regiment, or Royal Americans, had no lace on their uniforms. On the left is a grenadier in parade dress. The private soldier in the center is in full marching kit and the officer on the right is wearing his silver laced uniform.

The regimental coat for the 60th had no lace. It was constructed of red wool, with dark navy for the lining, cuffs, and lapels. The cuffs were slashed, and the lapels were square cut. The cuffs may have been from seven to seven and a quarter inches long, and the lapelS had six buttons each. There were twenty-eight, seven-eighths-inch buttons on the coat. Officers' uniforms were laced in silver braid.[84]

In 1757, the regiment appears to have received flannel waistcoats. These may have been sleeved waistcoats. A deserter report cites a soldier of the 60th wearing a red jacket with his regimental. Also in October, Lord Loudon wrote to the Duke of Cumberland that the Royal Americans were to have issued, flannel waistcoats.[85]

Other adaptations were demonstrated in 1758 and 1759. The 60th was to be issued woolen blue leggings. Enough blue wool could not be found at Albany, so green was substituted. These were trimmed and tied in red. "Received 9 pieces of cloth containing 209 yards to make 334 pairs of leggins 5/8 yard each, to the generals company 27; to Col. Haldimand, 23; to the Major's Company, 30; to the Grenadiers, 28; to Capt. Steiners, 25; to Capt. Prevost, 27; to Capt. Parkins, 12; to Capt. Wilymoz 15; to Capt. Dusez's, 25; to Capt. Burnards, 26."[86]

In late war, there is an excellent documentation of what the Royal American grenadier and the other regulars were issued. This is a very extensive list of clothing, gear, and equipment that should set a prime example of the full kit for the regulars. "Regimental coat with hooks, eyes, waistcoat, breeches, hat,

---

[84] Dr. Todd Harburn and Scott Stephenson, *Of Scarlet and Blue, The 60th Royal American Regimental Coat, 1755-1768* (n.p., 1984). Photocopy in Author's Private Collection, Houghton Lake, Mich.

[85] Pargellis, 401; *N.J. Documents,* 20: 90-91.

[86] Zaboly, *Descriptions,* 1: 16; Scott Stephenson, "Gaiters, Leggings, or Spatterdashes," *Standing Orders British Regular Regiments 1754-1764 Newsletter,* vol. 1 #5, May 1, 1989, 5; Lawson, 3: 212.

cockade, button, loop, hair string, shirt, stock with buckle, knee buckles, stockings, garters, shoes with buckles, firelock, sling, hammer cap, stopper, waist belt, hanger, sword knot, scabbard, bayonet and scabbard, tomahawk, cover, cartridge pouch with belt, buckles, match case, 24 rounds, brush, wire, worm, turnkey, oil bottle, rag, 2 flints and steel, knapsack with strap and buckles, containing; 2 shirts, 2 stocks, 2 pair stockings, a pair summer breeches, pair shoes, clothes brush, pair shoe brushes, black ball, pair leggins and garters, handkerchief, 2 combs, knife and spoon; haversack with; six days provisions, blanket strap and garters, canteen with string and stopper with water; all complete weighing just over sixty-three pounds."[87]

MONTGOMERY'S HIGHLANDERS, THE 77TH REGIMENT OF FOOT was raised in 1757, and by 1759, they were at Lake George (see Fig. 26). This unit at recruitment wore red, red-faced regimentals. But by 1759, their coats were red, faced dark green. The facings were round cuffs and large round collars. This regiment had no lacing, but officers ornamented their clothing with silver lace. The cut of the uniform was patterned after that of the 42nd Regiment.

Along with regimentals, men received waistcoats, highland bonnets, shirts, kilts similar to the government sett, harlequin hose, and shoes. For gear, the 77th were equipped like the Royal Highland Regiment (see Appendices 14, 15 and 16).[88]

ROYAL ARTILLERY. Starting in 1756, units of the Royal Artillery were stationed in the corridor (see Fig. 27). Unlike the other regulars, artillery uniform coats were dark navy with red facings. The cut of the coat was aligned with other

---

[87] Dr. Todd Harburn to Brenton C. Kemmer, 1994, "Necessary's for a Co. Of Grenadiers upon a March, Aug. 28, 1762." Papers of Henry Bouquet (Reel 11) ADD MSS 21648 p. 341, British Library, Photocopy, Author's Private Collection, Houghton Lake, Michigan.

[88] Spring and Bray, 3: 6, 16, 18; Embleton, part 1, 22; *Ibid.*, part 3, 42; Lawson, 2: 74.

Fig. 26. The 77th Regiment of Foot was uniformed and accoutered similarly to the Royal Highland Regiment, but without lace as shown by the soldier on the left in marching kit. The officer on the right is attired in full highland fashion with his broad sword, dirk, and sporran.

Fig. 27. The Royal Artillery was stationed at all the British forts in the corridor. On the left is a private soldier and on the right is his officer in a gold-laced uniform, gorget, and aguillette on his right shoulder.

regulars, but the facings were straight cut, and the cuffs were round. The coat pocket and arm flaps were rectangular with four buttons each. Officers laced their uniforms in gold. To distinguish ranks, officers wore gold aguillettes, sergeants wore two gold shoulder knots, corporals wore two white shoulder knots, and bombardiers wore one white shoulder knot.

Waistcoats were red with scalloped pockets. Officers laced their waistcoats in gold, and soldiers' waistcoats, until 1758, were laced in yellow wool tape. Looping was square. The artillery was also issued red breeches, shirts, stocks, hose, dress and marching gaiters, garters, shoes, and tricorns.

For gear, artillery men were given haversacks, canteens, knapsacks, and blankets. Fuzils and belly boxes were issued until 1759. Specified equipment and gear was also issued to the companies for the cannons, the primary emphasis of this unit. This varied depending on the type of gun, emplacement, and defensive or offensive priority.[89]

The Royal Navy started arriving in the Lake George–Lake Champlain Corridor in 1757 (see Fig. 28). These first arrivals were sailors placed under the supervision of lieutenants of the 35th Regiment of Foot. There were no standard uniforms for sailors in that century. Most of them wore useful, traditional maritime clothing. Men often went barefoot on board ships, but on land, shoes would have been worn with hose. Shirts were issued in white and checked, and neckerchiefs were popular. The majority of sailors did not wear breeches, but rather linen slops for ease of movement at their work. Some wore slops as overalls to protect their breeches. Other sailors popularly wore a type of canvas linen apron skirt, similar to the cut of a kilt. This apron was worn to protect the other garments. Waistcoats and sleeved short jackets were common. These were short in style, without cuffs. They

---

[89] May, plate G1 and p. 47; *Morier* #73; Lawson, 2: 102-03, 184, 85.

Fig. 28. There was no uniform for the Royal Navy except for the officers. In the center is a captain in his gold-laced uniform. The two sailors are dressed in traditional sailor's dress. Notice the slops and hats on the men. The sailor on the right is wearing the popular short sailor's jacket.

ranged in color but navy, dark brown, and red were popular. Hats varied from wide-brimmed, narrow-brimmed, painted canvas or tarpaulin hats, workman's caps and tricorns, to wool knit caps. Narrow-brimmed black felt, painted canvas tarpaulin and knit caps were favorites.

Sailors usually carried a canvas sea bag for their belongings, but many, once at the front, were also issued haversacks, canteens, knapsacks, muskets, and cartridge boxes. The traditional side arm, the cutlass, was carried by most.

In 1758, the first Royal Naval officer, Captain Loring, arrived. His men were uniformed. Their clothing was cut similar to the other regulars. Senior officers wore a navy blue regimental with white lapels and cuffs; junior captains wore blue coats with blue lapels, commanders wore blue coats, lapels, and cuffs; lieutenants wore blue coats with no lace. All officers except lieutenants laced their uniforms in gold braid. Senior officers wore white waistcoats, and the other officers wore blue. All officers wore blue breeches. Tricorns, hose, and shoes were standard.[90]

---

[90] May, p. 44; Keith Wilbur, *Pirates and Patriots* (Conn.: The Globe Pequot Press, 1984) 32.

Fig. 29 These Native American Allies are, left to right: Oneida, Mohican, and Mohawk. The Oneida is painted, tattooed and pierced as was their tradition. The Mohican is dressed as ordered in his native fashion. The Mohawk is clad in traditional dress, and one of the typical hair and tattoo designs of his tribe. These are the three major allied Indian tribes who fought with the British Army.

Part VI:

__INDIAN ALLIES__

Native Americans were another important fighting ally of the British army. Although limited, Indian assistance was available to the British in this war. Woodland warriors were essential to North American warfare. Natives were used as individual groups of warriors, as soldiers within the provincial regiments, and as companies within ranger units. There were only four basic tribes assisting the British in the Lake George–Lake Champlain Corridor: the Mohicans, Oneidas, Mohawks, and the Mohegans (see Fig. 29).

THE MOHAWKS were one of the first tribes to see battle in the corridor in 1755. Following King Hendrick, the Mohawk sachem, they were the primary allies at the Battle of Lake George. The Mohawks remained very loyal because of their close location to Lake George and the encouragement of William Johnson, Superintendant of Indian Affairs. Sir William had further enhanced the relations with that tribe by marrying a Mohawk. His home, as well, was in the heart of the Mohawk Valley. Johnson ordered the Mohawks and other Indian allies to wear a red fillet (band) on their head so allies would be distinguished from enemy Indians. In later war, Indians were ordered to attach a red garter to their musket barrel.[91]

This tribe wore center-seamed, woodland Indian moccasins and wool, center-seamed leggings to cover their legs. A short apron or breechclout was worn to cover the loins. At times this may have been their only clothing. Often, Mohawks wore shirts, coats, or coats without a shirt. The primary covering or

---

[91] Hill, 99-100; *Moneypenny*, 5/16/58.

garment was simply a blanket, usually black. Heads were not covered. Many Mohawk warriors wore their hair short and shaved the front of their heads from ear to ear.

Body adornments were common. Tattooing was quite standard. All parts of the body were tattooed in geometrics. Facial tattoos were also common. Often, a crescent was tattooed in front of the ear, and four to six elongated triangles radiated out from the crescent. Another common facial tattoo was a crescent descending off the corners of the mouth to the chin. Often, there were perpendicular lines tattooed within these crescents.

Ear and nose mutilation was common. Most Mohawk warriors had slit earlobes that had been stretched open and hung down one-half inch to two inches. Within these large piercings, glass beads, feathers, silver and wampum were commonly hung. Noses were pierced and adorned as well.

Most Mohawks were equipped with a scalping knife hung around the neck by a ribbon. Other weapons and gear carried included a musket, a bag to carry cartridges or loose ball, a powder horn, tomahawk, and a blanket, often carried on a tumpline when not worn.[92]

THE ONEIDAS were the only other Iroquois that could sometimes be counted on as an ally to the British. As with the Mohawks, the Oneidas fought in Indian groups. The Oneidas wore the traditional center-seamed moccasins and leggings. These leggins had no side flaps and were woolen or leather.

---

[92] Michael G. Johnson, *American Woodland Indians,* Men at Arms Series (London: Osprey Publishing, 1990) 8; James F. O'Neil II, ed. *Their Bearing is Noble and Proud, A Collection of Narratives Regarding the Appearance of Native Americans from 1740-1815* (Dayton, Ohio: J.T.G.S. Publishing, 1995) 18, 41, 57, 73, 85; Hill, 72, 73, 78, 99-100, 171; James T. Flexner, *Mohawk Baronet, A Biography of Sir William Johnson* (New York: Syracuse University Press, 1979) 123, 140-41, 144-45, 46, 153, 181, 192; Parkman, 169; S.H.P. Pell, *Fort Ticonderoga, A Short History* (Ticonderoga, N.Y.: Fort Ticonderoga Museum, 1987) 37.

Most of these men wore shirts (which they rarely changed for 6-8 months at a time), and wool wrapped around their loins, forming a little skirt. If more warmth was wanted, a red or black blanket was used to wrap up in.

The hair was plucked except for a tuft the size of a coin on the top-back of the head. The head was painted red, and feathers and beads were twisted and braided together in the hair. Ears were mutilated, hanging almost to the shoulders, and adorned with silver and beads. The nose was pierced, and red and black feathers hung from the nostrils. Warriors' faces were painted in one inch horizontal bands of white, red, black, blue, green and yellow, according to personal preference.

The Oneidas were well-equipped for battle. They carried muskets, ammunition bags and powder horns. A tomahawk was carried over the shoulder on a leather strap, and a dagger was carried in a belt worn around the waist. An embroidered traveling pouch held personal belongings, and each man carried his blanket on a tumpline.[93]

THE STOCKBRIDGE MOHICANS of Massachusetts and the Mohegans of Connecticut were the most assimilated of the allied tribes. These men fought both in Indian bands within provincial regiments, and with the ranger units. The Mohicans wore European-style clothing, and lived in towns rather than Indian villages. They lived in clapboard houses rather than traditional bark dwellings. Many of these men attended church and school and utilized all aspects of political, colonial Massachusetts. Despite this, these two tribes were ordered to dress in their traditional Indian fashion for war in order to intimidate the enemy.

The Mohicans were issued shirts, bullet bags, powder horns, blankets, and muskets. They also wore center-seam moccasins and leggings. Hair styles varied; some wore a scalplock, some

---

[93] Michael M. Mooney ed., *George Catlin, Letters and Notes on the North American Indians* (New York: Gramercy Books, 1975) 1: 311; Michael Johnson, 8; O'Neil, 20, 61-62.

wore their hair short, and some, as ordered, grew their hair long. Tattooing and painting were done but do not seem common. Piercings do not seem to have been used. Other typical garments were breeches, hose, waistcoats, coats, and hats. Many units of Mohicans and Mohegans were issued the same equipment that was issued to their fellow rangers such as belts, axes, haversacks, shoes, canteens, cartridge boxes, and knapsacks or packs.[94]

Robert Rogers, who had extensive knowledge of the Indians in Northeastern America, wrote a good description of the generic military dress of the Native Americans.

Cut off or pull out all their hair except a spot the size of an English crown near the crown of the head, their beards and eyebrows totally destroyed. The lock left upon their head is divided into several parcels, each of which is stiffened and adorned with wampum, beads, and feathers of various shapes and hues, and the whole twisted, turned, and connected together till it takes a form much resembling the modern pompadour upon the top of their heads. Their heads are painted red down to the eyebrows, and sprinkled over with white down. The gristles of their ears are split almost quite round, and then distended with wire or splinters, so as to meet and tie together in the nap of their necks. These also are hung with ornaments, and have generally the figure of some bird or beast drawn upon them. Their noses are likewise bored, and hung with trinkets of beads, and their faces painted with divers colours, which are so disposed as to make an awful appearance. Their breasts are adorned with a gorget, or medal of brass, copper, or some other metal; and that horrid weapon the scalping-knife hangs by a string which goes round their necks.[95]

[94] Patrick Frazier, *Mohicans of Stockbridge* (Lincoln: University of Nebraska Press, 1992) xii, xiv: 112-113, 116-117, 124-125, 130, 139, 220; Steele, 85; *Fort Ticonderoga Bulletin*, vol. XV, p. 373, 7/4/59.

[95] Major Robert Rogers, *A Concise Account of North America* (London: J. Millan, Bookseller, near Whitehall, 1765) 277, 230.

Part VII:

AUXILIARY, BATEAUXMEN, AND WAGGONERS

Following all the forces was an entire army of auxiliary troops. People were needed for preparing paperwork, organizing, building, provisioning, equipping, supplying, fixing, fabricating, communicating, and seeing to the medical and spiritual needs of the troops (see Fig. 30). All regiments had adjutants and clerks. The adjutant basically was a personal secretary for the field commander, and the clerks were scribes at the company level. Overseers, adjutants, commissaries and their assistants, muster masters and their assistants, and sutlers were in charge of organizing, provisioning, supplying, and equipping the soldiers and regiments. For communication other than secretarial, direct commands were distributed by drum majors, pipe majors, drummers, pipers, and fifers, especially important in the noise and din of battle. For repair and fabrication, armorers (blacksmiths), armorers' assistants, and woodworkers were employed within the auxiliary corps. Surgeons, surgeons' mates, and surgeons' mates' assistants traveled with their respective units. These men saw to the ill and wounded. Each surgeon was supplied with a well-stocked medical chest, instruments, and tents or buildings for hospitals. **SPIRITUAL NEEDS.** For spiritual needs, the regiments were furnished with chaplains. In the regulars these men were military men, but in the colonial forces, these were civilian ministers. Though supplied with equipment and gear, the

Fig. 30. Here are two members of the army's auxiliary staff. The man on the right is a surgeon's mate who has brought a broken instrument to an armorer (left) for repair.

majority of these men were not supplied with clothing or uniforms but were paid well for their work.[96]

MERCHANTS were extremely important to the supplying of the army. These businessmen directly supplied the army and sutlers for regulation and non issued items (see Fig. 31). Everything not bought or manufactured in Europe had to be acquired from these colonial storekeepers. A look at some advertisements from these businesses provides a good view of army supply:

> *Greg and Cunningham: powder, shot, shoes, stockings, leather breeches for soldiers, Albany, 1758.*
>
> *Rowland De Paiba: bearskin, duffels, coatings, rateens, strouds [sic], coarse cloths, rose and striped blankets, gold and silver chain and cord, regimental lace suitable for all regiments. In Albany, ready laced hats, silver hilt swords, red morocco leather sword belts, buckskin stitched and fur gloves, mittens, yarn stockings, regimental buckles, white and checked shirts for soldiers, Albany, 1758.*
>
> *Alexander McLean: Scotch and English camblets [sic] fit for officers' cloaks, broad cloths, fine fuzees, swan skin half thicks fit for soldiers' winter waistcoats, Albany, 1758.*
>
> *To be sold by James Jarvis, hatter, in French Street, choice regimental silver lace, in particular the Royal American Regimental lace.*
>
> *Samuel Blodget: blue broadcloth lapeled coats of various sizes, kersey and frieze ditto., embossed serge and swan skin jackets, double breasted; blue and red half-thicks breeches, German serge, drugget and leather ditto.; checked and ozanbrig [sic] trousers, checked shirts, milled and worsted caps, shoes &c. &c., Boston, 1759.*
>
> *George Richy, Upholsterer and Tent Maker: makes field and tent beds, fitting for gentlemen of the army; all sorts of tents and marquees for campaign, and all sorts of mattresses fitting for the sea or land service.* [97]

---

[96] Kemmer, *Freemen*, 53-54, 76, 78, 81-83, 86-87.
[97] Zaboly, *Descriptions*, 19; Kemmer, *Freemen*, 47.

Fig. 31. Pictured here is Samuel Blodget, one of the regiments' sutlers, or storekeepers who followed the army. Each regiment of the British Army had sutlers to supplement their King's or colony's stores. Both the regiments and individual soldiers purchased items from these merchants. Notice his wall tent, fly, and his stores for sale.

WAGONERS AND BATEAUX MEN. Wagons, carts and bateaux were employed to transport troops, equipment and gear. In the early war in the corridor, wagoners were issued clothing and equipment only if they were attached to the artillery (see Fig. 32). In that case, they were issued white frocks (work shirt or smocks) with the letters GR painted in red on the back. Later in the war the crown saw the importance of equipping these civilians, and supplying them became regular. The army had notoriously experienced many problems with the supply lines and constantly had to attach armed covering units to all wagon parties heading into and up the corridor. Hence, in 1759, it was ordered that wagoners and drivers of ox teams be organized into companies under officers and be well-clothed and supplied with a good firelock, shot bag, powder horn, cover for the lock of their gun, and a good blanket.[98]

---

[98] Lawson, 2: 187, 209; Zaboly, *Descriptions,* 10.

Fig. 32. The wagoner on the left is attached to the Royal Artillery. This can be distinguished by the red GR painted on the back of his workman's smock. The other wagoners had no type of uniform. Notice the blanket, powder horn, shot bag, and firelock issued to the center man. This arming and accoutering permitted wagoners to protect themselves instead of having extensive covering parties assigned to their movements.

Fig. 33. Like wagoners, the bateaux men were not uniformed, as shown by these three bateaux men. Notice the bateau man on the right standing guard with his issued firelock (notice the cover for the lock), bayonet, cartridge box, and hair-on knapsack.

Unlike wagoners, bateaux men had been organized into units by 1756. That year, William Shirley had Lt. Col. John Bradstreet recruit and organize two thousand men into companies of fifty men each (see Fig. 33). Each man was issued a good firelock, powder horn, shot bag, cover for the lock of his musket, a hatchet and a blanket. By 1758, Bradstreet and his men were an armed force, moving the army and fighting at the Battle of Ticonderoga with them. Then, in 1759, Amherst ordered the companies to have one captain and a lieutenant. Along with the previously listed equipment, he specified that each man was to be well-clothed. Some of the bateaux companies were supplied by the colonies. Massachusetts in 1759, for example, furnished 25 small arms, 48 cartouch boxes, 48 knapsacks, 30 powder horns, and 48 blankets for bateaux service.[99]

---

[99] *Journal of the House of New Hampshire,* 397; Lawson, 3: 208; Bartlett, 12; William Nelson, 331; Zaboly, *Descriptions*, 9.

Part VIII:

<u>DIVERSITY</u>

Great diversity was apparent in King George's army in the Lake George–Lake Champlain Corridor throughout the Seven Years' War. This was an army of Redcoats, Yankees, and their Allies. These men from England, Scotland and Ireland, with other recruits of German and Swiss ancestry, cemented with Americans from Massachusetts, Connecticut, New York, New Hampshire, New Jersey and Rhode Island; and were assisted by the Mohawks, Oneidas, Mohegans, and Mohicans, united in their quest to drive the French, Canadians and their allies from North America. Struggling with supply lines, arguing colonies, and Crown administration, the British commanders utilized every means, auxiliary person, camp follower, and warfare possible to attain their ultimate success.

For six consecutive years, the route of war engraved its presence on the Lake George–Lake Champlain Corridor. Armies of redcoats, provincials, rangers, light infantry and natives received uniforms, gear, equipment, tentage, and provisions from Europe and the colonies. This had been a true test of the armies of colonial America.

With the fairly new 1751 Uniform Warrant, the redcoats received their madder red, coated uniforms, learned from the Americans, and began to modify and redesign clothing, gear and equipment to the wooded terrain of the New World.

The Yankees, without standing armies, drew from their colonial trainbands and produced tens of thousands of wool-clad provincial troops. Few of these men had formal training or woodland warfare experience, but they proved themselves adept at learning, and tenured their fellow soldiers. Shrouded in blue, these citizen soldiers distinguished their appearance with accents of brown, gray, green, and red. The diversity of provincial troops was almost never ending, varying from rangers to provincial grenadiers.

Although small in numbers, the Native Americans took their understanding of the natural terrain of the Lake George–Lake Champlain Corridor, and their distinctive dress, and provided the model for woodland warfare for the army. Although their appearance was thought hideous by most Redcoats and Yankees alike, the Indians of Oneida, the Mohawk Valley, and western Massachusetts and Connecticut were irreplaceable as intimidators and allies.

Just as the Lake George–Lake Champlain Corridor was the key to the success of the conquest of North America, the successful uniforming of the British Army was paramount. Without the issuance of the necessities of a soldier, the success of a military campaign cannot be fulfilled. Thus, the superiority of the supply of this army of Redcoats, Yankees, and Allies, concretely culminated in the success of King George's Armies in America.

> *For promoting this great and important End, it is hereby published and made known, that every able-bodied effective Man that shall voluntary [sic] enlist in one of the Regiments, ordered to be raised for the Purpose aforesaid, and shall furnish himself with suitable Clothes, a Powder-Horn, and Shot-Bag, as aforesaid, he is to be supplied with the Same by his Captain out of the aforesaid Bounty, and the Remainder (if any be) to be paid him.*[100]

---

[100] "A Proclamation by His Majesty King George for the Raising of a Provincial Army," 1758. Photocopy, courtesy of Jerry Olson, in Author's Private Collection, Houghton Lake, Mich.

MARCHING ORDER and PARADE DRESS
Clothing, Gear and Equipment

Compiled by Brenton C. Kemmer - from:
Cecil C. P. Lawson, *A History of the Uniforms of the British Army*,
vol. 2. (London: Peter Davies, 1941.)

MARCHING ORDER

Hair tied; tricorn, trimmed, cockade, looped, and buttoned; shirt of the day and neck covering; breeches; hose; shoes, officers in most regiments to wear boots; brown or black gaiters according to regiment; waistcoat; regimental buttoned across the chest to the waist showing lapels turned back at top, waist belt worn outside over the waist of coat; belt and frog worn over the coat at the waist or over the shoulder as ordered; cartridge box worn on the right under the shoulder strap on the left shoulder passing under the waist belt in front and over in the back - wire and brush attached; sword or axe; bayonet; scabbards for all edged weapons; musket, sling, and tools (worm, wire, brush, turnkey, oil bottle, rag); cowhide knapsacks on left side near back; blanket rolled up, tied with garters, under straps of knapsacks; canteen on left side; haversack on right side. All to be in good working order. (Subject to regimental distinctions and order.)

Cartridge box to be full; canteen to have water; haversack contains food; knapsack to contain, extra clothing, clothes brush, shoe brushes, black ball, and personal belongings. (Contents subject to regimental orders and length and purpose of expedition.)

PARADE DRESS

Clean; hair dressed, combed, tied, and for some regiments powdered; tricorn, trimmed, cockade, looped, and buttoned; white shirt and neck covering; breeches; hose; shoes; white gaiters; garters; waistcoat; regimental with skirts turned back and lapels buttoned down; belt and frog under the coat; cartridge box, loose and over the coat; sword or axe; bayonet; scabbards for all edged weapons; musket sling, and tools (worm, wire, brush, turnkey, oil bottle, rag). (Some regiments, such as Highland regiments had other requirements as well.) All to be neat clean and serviceable.

Appendix 2:

SMALL CLOTHES

Regiment	Color of Small Clothes
1st Regiment of Foot	Red waistcoat/blue breeches
17th Regiment of Foot	Red
27th Regiment of Foot	Red
35th Regiment of Foot	Red
42nd Regiment of Foot	Red waistcoat/kilt
44th Regiment of Foot	Red
47th Regiment of Foot	Red
48th Regiment of Foot	Red
55th Regiment of Foot	Red
60th Regiment of Foot	Red waistcoat/blue breeches
77th Regiment of Foot	Red waistcoat/kilt
80th Regiment of Foot	Brown
Royal Artillery	Red
Royal Navy	White
New York Independents	Possibly Red
Massachusetts Regiment	Red/some blue breeches
Connecticut Regiment	Red
New Jersey Regiment	Red waistcoat/blue breeches
New York Regiment	Red waistcoat/blue breeches
Rhode Island Regiment	NA
New Hampshire Regiment	NA
Partridge's Rangers	NA
Dunn's Rangers	Green under jacket / buckskin breeches
Putnam's Rangers	Green waistcoat
Rogers' Rangers	varied
Sailors	NA
Bateaux Men	NA
Waggoners	NA

Appendix 3:

REGIMENTAL LACE

Regiment	Regimental Lace
1st Regiment of Foot	White/square loops
17th Regiment of Foot two	White/two gray zigzags, inside of green stripes/bastion loops
27th Regiment of Foot	White/yellow stripe, between two blue zigzags/square loops
35th Regiment of Foot	White/yellow zigzag, between a yellow and red zigzag/square loops
42nd Regiment of Foot	White/two red stripes/bastion loops
44th Regiment of Foot	White/yellow stripe, between a blue and black zigzag/diamond on lapel/others bastion loops
47th Regiment of Foot	White/yellow diamonds between two black zigzags /square loops
48th Regiment of Foot	White/yellow stripe between a green scroll and green stripe /square loops on coat/diamond on waistcoat
55th Regiment of Foot	Yellow/square loops
60th Regiment of Foot	NA
77th Regiment of Foot	NA
80th Regiment of Foot	NA
Royal Artillery	Yellow on waistcoats early war/square loops

No regimental lace on other regiments.

Appendix 4:

REGIMENTAL LACE / DIAGRAMS

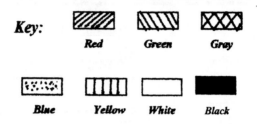

Key: Red Green Gray

Blue Yellow White Black

1ST Regiment of Foot

17th Regiment of Foot

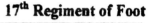

27th Regiment of Foot

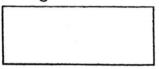

35th Regiment of Foot

42nd Regiment of Foot

44th Regiment of Foot

47th Regiment of Foot

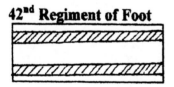

48th Regiment of Foot

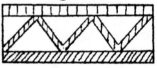

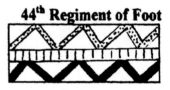

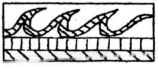

Appendix 5:

OFFICER'S BRAID/LACE

Regiment	Braid/Lace Color
1st Regiment of Foot	Gold
17th Regiment of Foot	Silver
27th Regiment of Foot	Silver
35th Regiment of Foot	Silver
42nd Regiment of Foot	Gold
44th Regiment of Foot	Silver
47th Regiment of Foot	Silver
48th Regiment of Foot	Gold
55th Regiment of Foot	Gold
60th Regiment of Foot	Silver
77th Regiment of Foot	Silver
80th Regiment of Foot	Possibly Gold
Royal Artillery	Gold
Royal Navy	Gold
New York Independents	NA / Possibly Gold
Massachusetts Regiment	Gold
Connecticut Regiment	Silver
New Jersey Regiment	Gold
New York Regiment	Gold
Rhode Island Regiment	NA
New Hampshire Regiment	NA
Partridge's Rangers	NA
Dunn's Rangers	NA
Putnam's Rangers	NA
Rogers' Rangers	Silver
Sailors	NA/*Naval officers Gold*
Bateaux Men	NA
Wagoners	NA

Appendix 6:

FACING COLORS

Regiment	Facing Color
1st Regiment of Foot	Blue
17th Regiment of Foot	Grayish-white
27th Regiment of Foot	Buff
35th Regiment of Foot	Orange
42nd Regiment of Foot	Buff / after *1758-Blue*
44th Regiment of Foot	Yellow
47th Regiment of Foot	White
48th Regiment of Foot	Buff
55th Regiment of Foot	Green
60th Regiment of Foot	Blue
77th Regiment of Foot	Red / *1759-Green*
80th Regiment of Foot	NA early; *1760's-Red Orange*
Royal Artillery	Blue/Faced Red
Royal Navy	Officers only-Blue/Faced White & Blue
New York Independents	Red/Faced Green & Green/Faced Green
Massachusetts Regiment	Blue/Faced Red & *1759-blue, red, green*
Connecticut Regiment	Red/Faced Yellow/late Blue/Faced Red
New Jersey Regiment	Blue/Faced Red
New York Regiment	Blue/Faced Red & *1759-Drab/FacedDrab*
Rhode Island Regiment	NA
New Hampshire Regiment	NA
Partridge's Rangers	NA
Dunn's Rangers	Green/Faced Green - *This was sleeveless*
Putnam's Rangers	Brown/Faced ?
Rogers' Rangers	Green/Faced Green - & some Gray/Faced ?
Sailors	NA
Bateaux Men	NA
Wagoners	NA

Appendix 7:

EXAMPLES OF MARKINGS
Clothing, Gear, and Equipment

17th Regiment of Foot, Colonel's company, rack number 25, King's issue, markings of shirts.

↑ **17th Regt.**

GR   A/25

47th Regiment of Foot, Major's company, rack number 42, King's issue, markings of breeches, waistcoats, regimentals, watch coats, and hats on tab of tape stitched to garment.

↑   **47th Regt.**

GR   C/42

1st Battalion, 42nd Regiment of Foot, Fourth Captain's company, rack number 33, King's issue, markings of haversacks, knapsacks, snapsacks, packs, and canteens.

↑ **1st Batt. 42nd Regt.**

GR   G/33

New Jersey Regiment, Lt. Col. Company, rack number 15, colony's issue, markings of belts, frogs, and slings

NJ
B/15

55th Regiment of Foot, 2nd Captain's company, rack number 17,
King's issue,markings of blankets.

↑ **55th Regt.**
GR   E/17

1st Regiment of Foot, 1st Captain's company, <u>Mess number</u> 6,
King's issue, markings of tents and camp kettles.

↑ **1st Regt.**
GR   D/6

Below are other examples of markings:

↑**27th Regt.**   ↑**35th Regt.**   ↑ **44th Regt.**
GR   F/35   GR   I/22   GR   J/27

↑**48th Regt.**   ↑ **2nd Batt. 60th Regt.**   ↑ **77th Regt.**
GR A/38   GR   H/12   GR   D/18

↑ **80th Regt.**   ↑**3rd Batt. RA**   **2nd Conn.**
GR   C/12   GR   C/18   C/36

<u>**NY**</u>   **3rd Mass.**   <u>**RI**</u>
E/23   C/46   B/6

Appendix 8:

Clothing and Gear Issuance, Massachusetts Regiments Lake George - Lake Champlain Corridor

Clothing Issue

[Not all of the following may have been issued every year]

Regimental coat, waistcoat, breeches, white shirt, neck covering, tricorn-cockade-ferreting-button, stockings, garters, shoes and buckles, checked shirt, great coats for guard.

Gear Issue

[Not all of the following may have been issued every year]

Musket (often Brown Bess) with sling-hammer cap-stopper-brush-wire-worm-turnkey-oil bottle-rag, bayonet, sword or cutlass and sword knot or axe, belt and frog, scabbards for all edged weapons, cartridge box with belt and buckle or bullet bag, powder horn, haversack, canteen or wooden bottle, knapsack or snapsack, blanket with garters, tumpline.

Each mess also was issued: camp axe, tent, kettle, and other cooking and cleaning supplies.

Appendix 9:

Clothing and Gear Issuance, Connecticut Regiments
Lake George-Lake Champlain Corridor

Clothing Issue

[Not all of the following may have been issued every year]

Regimental coat, waistcoat, breeches, white shirt and neck covering, tricorn-cockade-ferreting-button, stockings, garters, shoes and buckles, checked shirt, checked trousers, leggings, great coat for guard.

Gear Issue

[Not all of the following may have been issued every year]

Musket (often Brown Bess) with sling-hammer cap-stopper-brush-wire-worm-turkey-oil bottle-rag, bayonet, cartridge box, shot bag, powder horn, axe, sword and knot or cutlass, scabbards for all edged weapons, canteen, haversack, knapsack, blanket with garters.

Each mess also was issued: camp axe, tent, kettle, and other cooking and cleaning supplies.

Appendix 10:

Clothing and Gear Issuance, New York Regiments Lake George - Lake Champlain Corridor

Clothing Issue

[Not all of the following may have been issued every year]

Regimental coat, waistcoat, breeches, canvas trousers, shirt, tricorn, stockings, shoes and buckles, great coats for guard.

Gear Issue

[Not all of the following may have been issued every year]

Musket (often Brown Bess) with sling-hammer cap-stopper-brush-wire-worm-turnkey-oil bottle-rag, bayonet, hatchet, belt and frog, scabbards for all edged weapons, cartridge box with belt and buckle or bullet bag, powder horn, haversack, canteen, blanket.

Each mess also was issued: camp axe, tent, kettle, and other cooking and cleaning supplies.

Appendix 11:

Clothing and Gear Issuance, New Jersey Regiments
Lake George - Lake Champlain Corridor

Clothing Issue

[Not all of the following may have been issued every year]

Regimental coat, waistcoat, wool and ticken breeches, white shirt, neck covering, tricorn-cockade-yellow ferreting-button, stockings, garters, white gaiters, shoes and buckles, checked shirt, great coats for guard.

Gear Issue

[Not all of the following may have been issued every year]

Musket (often Brown Bess) with sling-hammer cap-stopper-brush-wire-worm-turnkey-oil bottle-rag, bayonet, hatchet, belt and frog, scabbards for all edged weapons, cartridge box with belt and buckle, powder horn, haversack, canteen, knapsack, blanket.

Each mess also was issued: camp axe, tent, kettle, and other cooking and cleaning supplies.

Appendix 12:

Clothing and Gear Issuance, Dunn's Rangers
Lake George - Lake Champlain Corridor

Clothing Issue

[Not all of the following may have been issued every year]

Green under jacket, gray-lapelled kersey waistcoat to wear over jacket, buckskin breeches, shirt, leather cap, stockings, leggings, shoes and buckles.

Gear Issue

[Not all of the following may have been issued every year]

Musket (often Brown Bess) with sling-hammer cap-stopper-brush-wire-worm-turnkey-oil bottle-rag, hatchet, belt and frog, scabbards for all edged weapons, cartridge box with belt and buckle, powder horn, haversack, canteen, knapsack, blanket, tent.

Appendix 13:

Clothing and Gear Issuance, Rogers' Rangers
Lake George - Lake Champlain Corridor

Clothing Issue

[Not all of the following may have been issued every year]

Green regimental or gray duffel coat or workman's-hunting shirt (uniform to each company), waistcoat, breeches, shirt, tricorn-Highland bonnet-felt round hat-or felt jockey cap, stockings, leggings, moccasins, shoes and buckles.

Gear Issue

[Not all of the following may have been issued every year]

Musket (carbines, special muskets, often Brown Bess, blunder buss) with sling-hammer cap-stopper-brush-wire-worm-turnkey-oil bottle-rag, hatchet, cutlass, belt and frog, scabbards for all edged weapons, cartridge box with belt and buckle or bullet bag, powder horn, haversack, canteen, knapsack, blanket, tumpline, tent.

Appendix 14:

Clothing and Gear Issuance, 1st, 17th, 27th, 35th, 44th, 47th, 48th, 60th Regiments of Foot
Lake George - Lake Champlain Corridor

Clothing Issue

[Not all of the following may have been issued every year]

Regimental coat with hook and eyes, waistcoat, breeches with knee buckles, white shirt, neck covering, hair tie, tricorn with ferreting-loops-cockade-button, stockings, white and marching gaiters, garters and buckles, shoes and buckles, fatigue shirt, forage cap, great coats for guard; some regiments issued leggings.

Gear Issue

[Not all of the following may have been issued every year]

Musket (Brown Bess) with sling-hammer cap-stopper-brush-wire-worm-turnkey-oil bottle-rag, bayonet, sword and sword knot or axe, belt and frog, scabbards for all edged weapons, cartridge box with belt and buckles, haversack, canteen and string and stopper, knapsack with black ball - clothes brush - shoes brushes-and personal belongings such as comb-spoon-knife-handkerchief-and extra clothing, blanket with garters (some issued tumpline).

Each mess also was issued: camp axe, tent, kettle, and other cooking and cleaning supplies.

Appendix 15:

Clothing and Gear Issuance, 42nd, 77th Regiments of Foot
Lake George - Lake Champlain Corridor

Clothing Issue

[Not all of the following may have been issued every year]

Regimental coat, waistcoat, plaid and little kilt, sailcloth breeches, white shirt, neck covering, hair tie, highland bonnet with tassel-cockade-button-bear fur, stockings harlequin or tartan, red tape for garters, leggings, shoes and buckles, checked shirt, great coats for guard.

Gear Issue

[Not all of the following may have been issued every year]

Musket (Brown Bess) with sling-hammer cap-stopper-brush-wire-worm-turnkey-oil bottle-rag (1759 pistols), bayonet, broad sword and sword knot or axe, baldrick, scabbards for all edged weapons, cartridge box with belt and buckles, haversack, canteen and string and stopper, knapsack with black ball - clothes brush - shoes brushes- and personal belongings such as comb-spoon-knife-handkerchief-and extra clothing, blanket with garters, tumpline (all leather straps to be black).

Each mess also was issued: camp axe, tent, kettle, and other cooking and cleaning supplies.

Appendix 16:

BRITISH MUSICIANS' COATS, DRUMS, FLAGS, CAMP COLORS, AND BELLS OF ARMS
Compiled by Brenton C. Kemmer - from:
Cecil C.P. Lawson, *A History of the Uniforms of the British Army,*
vol. 2. (London, Peter Davies, 1941.)

Musicians' Coats

Blue faced regiments: musician's coats = blue coat, faced-lined-lapelled red, laced with royal lace. The caps were similar to the grenadier caps but not stiff, hanging down in the back like a bag with a tassel on the end. The front was the facing color with a trophy of drums and arms embroidered on it. A drum was embroidered on the back band.

Other regiments: coat of their facing color, faced-lined-lapelled red, laced in regimental lace as directed by their colonel.

Drums

The front of the drum was painted in the regiment's facing color. The King's Cipher and Crown, and the number of the regiment under it to be painted on the front.

Colours/Flags

Each unit had two flags. The first was the great union or King's colours. The second flag was the regimental colour. This was a flag of the regiment's facing color with the union in the upper canton except those with facings of red or white. These were to be white with a red cross of St. George over the entire flag, with a small union in the upper corner. In the center of the regimental colours was the regiment's number in gold paint or embroidery. Roman numerals were used within a wreath of roses and thistles. The regiments that were allowed to use Royal devices or ancient badges placed them in the center and the number of the regiment in the upper corner.

Camp Colors

Camp colors were approximately eighteen inches square, of the facing color. The number of the regiment was painted or embroidered in roman numerals on them.

Bells of Arms

They were to be painted the same as the regimental drums.

Glossary

Abatis.__ Gate or fence of sharpened sticks. Usually a horizontal post with sharpened sticks protruding to make an impassable fence work.

Aguillett.__ Metallic looping worn on the shoulder of officers' coats to distinguish rank.

Armourer.__ A military blacksmith. Also *armorer*.

Artificer.__ A skilled man. Usually a skilled tradesman in building in the military.

Baldrick.__ A leather shoulder strap and carridge to carry a sword or axe.

Bandoleer.__ A way of carrying the blanket across the shoulder in a similar way as the earlier belts of cartridges were worn across the chest.

Bastion.__ A part of the fortification usually on a corner that projects out in order to better defend.

Bateau.__ French word for boat. In English military terms, a bateau was usually a double ended, flat bottomed boat. Lengths varied according to usage. Plural: *bateaux*.

Belly box.__ Small cartridge box worn on a belt around the waist. It consisted of a wooden block with pre-drilled holes and a leather flap. Used to carry pre-rolled ammunition.

Black ball.__ A pasty substance used to keep the black leather in a soldier's kit polished. Made of animal fat, pigment, and wax.

Blockhouse.__ A stand-alone fortified building.

Braid.__ Metallic lace worn on officers' clothing to distinguish rank.

Breastwork.__ A temporary breast-high fortification. Made from earth, log, fascines (bundles of sticks), gabions (earth filled baskets), or other materials found on site.

Breeches.__ Britches, or short, knee-length pants.

Brig.__ A two-masted, square-rigged vessel of about 200 tons.

Broad arrow.__ A marking used to designate King's ownership. This was an arrow painted, stamped, or branded on King's issued military items.

Bullet bag.__ Bag to carry bullets. Usually leather, many were probably just a drawstring bag.

Bullet pouch.__ A leather pouch or bag used to carry bullets or ammunition. Some historians believe this may have been another term for cartridge box or pouch.

Camblet.__ A wool or silk fabric, or combination of both, used often for cloaks. Also spelled **camlet**.

Camp followers.__ Women and children who followed the colonial armies and performed many duties such as cleaning, cooking, mending and nursing. Many, but not all camp followers were relatives of the soldiers, and some of the camp followers were prostitutes.

Cap.__ A skull-type cap worn by all of society. The most popular hat in this time period. Made of multiple triangular pieces of fabric sewn together with the large end being the bottom. This bottom was often rolled up in a cuff. Linen and wool were the most popular fabrics. All fabrics were used from coarse linen for workmen to fine silks for gentlemen.

Clothier.__ A maker and supplier of clothing.

Cockade.__ Black silk or linen ribbon worn under the looping of the soldier's hat secured by a regimental button. This was affixed to the left side of the hat.

Corporal's knot.__ A white worsted shoulder knot or loop worn on the left shoulder of the corporal's regimental coat to distinguish his rank. A few units such as Massachusetts were issued yellow knots.

Council of war.__ A council of officers or the military family, used to help with military decisions.

Cravat.__ Rectangular piece of fabric wrapped around the neck of the shirt; forerunner of the tie. Also called *necks*.

Drab.__ A dull, yellowish-green color.

Drugget.__ Heavy wool coating material.

Duffel.__ A heavy woolen fabric.

***Entrenchment.*__ A trenchwork usually with a breastwork for added protection.

***Equipment.*__ Items used in the performance of, or to assist in the living of a soldier, not related to battle or things usually carried by the soldier. Items issued to the mess or military unit.

***Escutcheon.*__ A decorative brass plate on the wrist of the military musket stock. This usually had markings on issued muskets.

***Facings.*__ The lapels, cuffs, and lining of the regimental coat.

***Ferreting.*__ White worsted tape stitched around the brim of the soldier's hat. Some units like the New Jersey laced their hats in yellow ferreting.

***Fillet.*__ A narrow strip of material often worn on the head as a band.

***Firelock.*__ The flintlock musket or soldier military gun. Usually the Brown Bess.

***Flesh brush.*__ A brush used by soldiers to dress meat by brushing the salt from their salted rations.

***Floating battery.*__ A raft or vessel designed low in the water to transport and be used as a firing platform for artillery.

***Forage cap.*__ Woolen hat made from scraps of old regimental clothing. Originally for holding foraged food. Used as a fatigue hat. Similar in cut to a night cap, hanging down to the shoulder. The body of the hat was the regimental coat's color and a band of facing-colored wool was attached. It was lined in linen and had a white tassel on the end. Some regiments may have had their regiment's number on the front.

Frieze.__ A thick, warm wool.

Frizzen.__ Part of the lock of the musket. A steel plate that when struck by the flint, falls and opens a pan filled with powder, showering sparks over the pan and igniting the charge.

Frog.__ A loop or several loops of leather affixed to the belt to work as a carriage for swords, axes, and bayonets. Also called a **hanger**.

Fuzil.__ Officer's or light infantry musket. Often designed after the Brown Bess but of smaller stature and smaller caliber. Also called *fuzee*.

Gaiters.__ Canvas tube cut and sewn to fit over the leg from the heel to the middle of the thigh. Gaiters buttoned closed by a series of buttons on the outside of the leg. Used to protect the leg and hose of the soldier.

Gear.__ Items carried and used by the soldier directly related to battle or his maneuvers. Items issued to a single soldier for his duty.

Gorget.__ Crescent shaped metal badge worn around the neck of officers to distinguish rank. Originally part of the suit of armor for protecting the neck. Many were embossed or engraved.

Grenadier.___ Originally a company of men in a regiment
whose duty it was to throw grenades. By the Seven
Years' War this elite company was used to showcase
the regiment, or to shock and intimidate the enemy.

Halberd.___ A sergeant's pole arm. Usually, an axe-type
weapon affixed to a long pole used by the sergeant as a
badge of rank, to be seen in battle, to direct his men,
and as a weapon. Primarily used as a ceremonial
weapon in this war.

Half thicks.___ A coarse, thick, napped, plain woven wool
(similar to frieze).

Hammer cap.___ A leather sheath fitting over the frizzen of
the musket's lock in order to stop it from sparking
incase of accidental shooting. Frizzen cover.

Hanoverian.___ Belonging to the Hanovers. The Kings of
Britain (George I, II, III) were of Havoverian, German
descent.

Hat company.___ Companies of a regiment who are not of an
elite unit. Originally, companies wearing the tricorn
hat, i.e., not grenadier or light infantry companies.

Haversack.___ A coarse linen bag on a shoulder strap used by
soldiers to carry food rations and eating utensils.

Kersey.___ A twill-woven, cheap, woolen, broadcloth.

Knapsack.___ A shoulder-slung bag used by the military to
carry extra clothing, equipment, and personal effects.
Usually made of brown cow, horse, or goat hide with
the hair on. The strap was leather with a brass buckle

and the bag closed with buckles and straps. Some were made of canvas linen and a few of leather.

Leggings.__ Tubes of wool or leather worn on the leg from heel to mid thigh to protect the leg and hose. Usually center seamed, but occasionally outside seamed.

Levies.__ Troops promised or raised for military service.

Loops or looping.__ Tape or lacing sewn around button holes on uniforms.

Madder.__ An orange-red color used in the British Army for their enlisted men's uniforms. The dye is derived from the root of the madder plant.

Mess.__ A group of soldiers who receive provisions and equipment as a unit. Usually 5-6 men were a mess. Sometimes called mess mates. They were issued food, and a tent, axe, and cooking kettle as a mess.

Mitre.__ A mitre cap or a grenadier's cap.

Oilcloth.__ Linen that was treated with linseed oil or painted with pigment to make it water-repellent.

Oilskin.__ A piece oilcloth used to cover something, usually a person, to keep dry.

Oznaburg.__ Heavy, coarse, linen canvas. Often used for tents or trousers. Also spelled *ozenbrig*.

Plaid.__ Kilt or fabric of belted plaid wrapped around the waist and often with the extra fabric folded over the shoulder. Typical highland dress.

Radow.__ A seven-sided floating gun battery. This low-riding, flat bottomed boat was pointed on the bow, forming a seven-sided polygon.

Rateen.__ A heavy wool fabric. Also spelled **ratteen**.

Regimental lace.__ Decorative wool lace or tape with a distinctive regimental pattern woven into it. The pattern was regulated by British Army Uniform Warrants. Used to distinguish regiments.

Sachem.__ A leader of Native American groups.

Serge.__ Middle weight, inexpensive, hard wearing, woolen twill.

Shalloon.__ Middle weight, inexpensive, hard wearing wool. Like modern challis.

Sloop.__ Boat with one mast.

Slops.__ Similar cut to breeches but the leg is left open and full. Slops varied in length. Typical sailor's dress.

Snapsack.__ Similar to a knapsack, but the bag is in the shape of a tube, sometimes tied off at the ends.

Spontoon.__ An officer's pole arm. A spear-type of weapon affixed to a long pole used by officers as a badge of rank, to be seen in battle, and as a weapon. Primarily used as a ceremonial weapon in this war. Also called an **espontoon**.

Stock.__ Linen neck covering that fastens in the back of the neck with buckles or ties.

***Subaltern.*__ A subordinate officer. Usually Ensigns and Lieutenants.

***Sutler.*__ Merchant hired to follow a regiment and supply it with wanted merchandise.

***Swivel gun.*__ A small caliber cannon mounted on a swivel and used on boats, ships, and fortifications.

***Sword knot.*__ Loop and tassel tied around the hilt of the sword in which the hand was passed through so as not to drop the weapon in battle. Mostly for decoration in this war. Soldiers' knots were of leather, officers' knots were usually crimson and gold or silver.

***Ticken.*__ A strong, tightly woven linen.

***Trainband.*__ The colonial militias. Men of each colony belonged to, and trained in their militias monthly.

***Tricorn.*__ Standard regimental hat or soldier's hat. A three-cornered or three-sided hat of black felt.

***Tumpline.*__ A leather strap used to carry items slung over the shoulders or chest. Often used to carry the blanket.

***Turnkey.*__ A tool similar to a screwdriver for use with the musket.

***Victuals.*__ Food or provisions.

***Waistcoat.*__ Vest-type garment square cut on the bottom hem. The normal waistcoat was sleeveless but the sleeved waistcoat did exist.

***Wampum.*__** Cylindrically shaped beads made from northern quahog shells, primarily found in New England waters.

***Watch coat.*__** Great coat or large woolen overcoat used for guard duty or standing watch.

***Whaleboat.*__** Double ended, round bottomed boat used for whaling. In the military this type of boat was used to carry primarily light troops because of its quickness compared to a bateau.

Index Of Names, Subjects And Places

Compare uniforms
worn by soldiers
today with the
Revolutionary
outfits.